LIVE A LIFE THAT IS
LIMITLESS

Create a life of total ease that is fulfilling, rewarding and fun!

By

John Swanepoel

Live a Life That is Limitless

FatBoyGinger Publishing
Tauranga, New Zealand

Copyright © 2015 by John Swanepoel.

All rights reserved. No part of this publication may be reproduced, distributed or transmitted in any form or by any means, including photocopying, recording, or other electronic or mechanical methods, without the prior written permission of the publisher, except in the case of brief quotations embodied in critical reviews and certain other noncommercial uses permitted by copyright law. For permission requests, write to the publisher, addressed "Attention: Permissions Coordinator," at the address below.

FatBoyGinger Publishing
P.O. Box 15119
Tauranga 3144
Bay Of Plenty
New Zealand
www.fatboyginger.com

Publisher's Note: This is self help work. Names, characters, places, and incidents are people who have helped the author and places and situations the author has experienced. Locales and public names are sometimes used for atmospheric purposes. Any resemblance to actual people the author does not know personally, living or dead, or to businesses, companies, events, institutions, or locales is completely coincidental.

Book Layout ©2013 BookDesignTemplates.com

Ordering Information:
Quantity sales. Special discounts are available on quantity purchases by corporations, associations, and others. For details, contact the "Special Sales Department" at the address above.

"Live a Life That is Limitless"
John Swanepoel – 1st ed.
ISBN 978-0-473-37790-8

John Swanepoel

This is dedicated to Connor and Chloe.
Thank you for choosing me.
Keep your choices light,
your journey filled with kindness,
gratitude, peace and calm.
May total allowance be your Truth.
May you remain loving caring and intelligent
without allowing abuse into your world.
And above all
Do What You Love, it is what you are here for.
you are amazing and dearly loved….

Live a Life That is Limitless

Acknowledgements
Gary M Douglas. Access Consciousness
Dr. Dain Heer. Access Consciousness
Dr. John Veltheim. PaRama Bodytalk System
And every other teacher I have had in my life.

Thank You All

John Swanepoel

INTRODUCTION

You are a limitless being who has been conditioned into a continuous state of distraction. The stories you are fed everyday help to maintain the belief that you have limited choices in life. That feeling you get that you don't quite fit into this world, is because you are here to help create a new one. You are a gorgeous humanoid with a beautiful sense of humour and an intolerance for lies. You hate violence, yet are unafraid. You are often ignored or unheard, as you explain how things are going to turn out. You distract yourself with technology occasionally peeping out at the insanity of the world around you. You are often accused of doing nothing, contributing nothing and taking everything. You are far more conscious and adaptable than your parents ever were at your age. You are loving, caring and intelligent, so you often attract people into your life who take advantage of you. You are intelligent enough to understand why and loving and caring enough

Live a Life That is Limitless

to forgive them which keeps them coming back for more. You are part of the crowd that will fund the change the world is craving. You are already looking for a different way of being so you can start living the limitless life you just can't seem to grasp.

When you believe you don't have a choice nothing changes. What are you not choosing in your life because someone told you it would not work for you or you are not good enough? What are you not choosing in your life because you are waiting to be told what to do? What are you not choosing in your life because you are afraid you will be wrong or you will fail? You have the ability to live a limitless life filled with ease, joy and abundance. If limitless was easy what would you choose?

Here is a little about what I believe and some of the more significant experiences I have had in my life so far. These experiences have helped me understand the challenges we go through in life are there to strengthen us and help us grow. I don't tend to mince my words I just call things as I see them. This is not usually meant to insult or shock you, I just don't see the point in fluffing around incase someone takes offence.

I am spiritual, not religious. I am not concerned with the labels you choose for yourself, what colour your skin is, who or what you choose to follow. Christian, Muslim, Buddhist, Taoist, Catholic, Mormon, Hindu, Sikh, Jehovah's Witness or any other belief system. I SEE YOU and wish you peace and total allowance through your life. To me you are an Infinite Being having a human experience. For that reason alone you are my brother or sister. I recognise those of you who choose differently to me have the right to do so. I honour those who choose kindness, gratitude, peace and calm, and will happily defend those who cannot defend themselves from anger, rage, fury and hate and I do this without reaction or prejudice.

I believe we have a soul that never dies. An infinite being enjoying the human experience through our bodies. I believe Karma are the lessons our soul is here to experience. Karma is ever changing and evolving, the foundations of which are like USB pen drives plugged into our DNA and external energy fields. Little software pro-

Live a Life That is Limitless

grammes that stop running when we have completed the last level of each lesson or become aware enough to disconnect the programme. I believe our infinite being knows everything there is to know, and gets to experience a fragment of that knowledge through our bodies.

Our bodies are living organic beings, continuous manifestations of how we used to think. Living organisms with their own levels of consciousness, more than capable of healing themselves when given the opportunity. Amazing biological processing units that love and support our souls unconditionally from the moment we are born to that instant our body chooses to die. Allowing our soul the opportunity to experience the lessons our everyday experiences create.

In 1991 when a returned home from serving with the British Forces in the first Gulf War, I met up with a friend of mine who was learning to read Tarot cards. She offered to do a reading for me. I agreed, not taking it seriously. During the reading she mentioned New Zealand would play an important role in my life, and that I would change careers quite quickly and be surrounded by women. I remember finding that very hard to believe. At that time there was no way I was leaving the Royal Marines, I still had sixteen years to serve and I enjoyed being a Commando. I had no immediate plans to visit any part of Australasia. New Zealand certainly was not on my radar. The only thing I knew about New Zealand was their national rugby team usually won. The nature of my job meant I was constantly travelling. We only ever had three weeks summer leave, so I didn't think the journey was worth it. Within three years of that reading I no longer wanted to be in the forces. I volunteered to move to the Commando Training Centre as a drill instructor to access the education programmes that would get me into university. I applied for redundancy in 1995 and left the Royal Marines the following year. Three months after leaving I started a physiotherapy degree surrounded by young women. Two years after qualifying as a physiotherapist and acupuncturist, I followed my girlfriend to New Zealand, and here I am fifteen years later, living with my two awesome children. For the past 11 years I have used an alternative health modality mostly practiced by women, with most of my patients being women. So I guess the reading my friend gave in 1991 was pretty spot on after all.

Live a Life That is Limitless

I was born in Matabele Land, Rhodesia now Zimbabwe, at the beginning of the end of colonial rule. A privileged little white boy in a segregated world. My mother had turned twenty a couple of weeks before I was born. I was her second child. She had been struggling to bring her oldest boy up on her own when she fell pregnant with me. She nursed me for five days before the Nuns put me up for adoption. While she was in the maternity home, her parents put my brother into the local children's home. By the time my mother got to the home the government had given him away too.

I was adopted at nine days old by a kind hearted Christian couple who gave me plenty of encouragement. My mother had been sent to Africa as a missionary where she met and married my father. I grew up not wanting for anything. We had a large house with an african servant who maintained the house and garden. He lived in the servants quarters at the back of the property during the week and went home to his family at weekends. As kids we went to Sunday school every week, sang in the children's choir and played in the children's church band. I remember being about four years old in one Sunday school class finding the story in Genesis a little hard to believe because no-one could give me a straight answer as to why the Bible didn't mention Tyrannosaurus Rex and all the other dinosaurs.

One of the earliest memories I have is standing in the morning sun at the foot of my parents bed taking off my own nappy. I remember how uncomfortable it felt and never used one again. At the age of three I was sexually abused for the first time. Later that year I took hold of the element of our portable electric fire, plugged it in and flicked the switch. My mother watched in horror from the kitchen screaming for me to stop. Fortunately the back of my hand was touching the fire guard so electricity shorted through the back of my hand preventing my death. I put the fire down and walked to the kitchen where my mother was freaking out. I don't remember any pain, it felt more like my hand had been wrapped in sellotape. Fortunately my grandma was there, she calmly but firmly told my mother to get the honey out of the cupboard, gently dipped my hand in the jar, wrapped it in a bandage and told my mum to take me to hospital. Over the next

Live a Life That is Limitless

seven years I had extensive surgery on my hand and continued to be abused. I became a prolific bed wetter and an angry insecure boy.

Rhodesian schools held Victorian principles based on the elite public school systems of the UK. Any violation of the rules resulted in the cane or manual labour, depending on who caught you. There was a deep pride and loyalty instilled for both school and country. It wasn't all bad, I have always been very independent and fiercely competitive. This combination brought me success especially in the water. I became an excellent swimmer, and was often asked to compete against kids two or three years older. Being a little white boy in Africa at the time was a huge adventure. School always finished a 1:05pm so we had plenty of time to play. Most of us had pools in our gardens so we took turns visiting friends, or rode our bikes into the bush on the outskirts of the city. During the rainy season we sometimes swam in the local rivers or road the rapids on tractor tire inner tubes. In the dry season we climbed down into the cities storm drains and explored the local underground networks.

This was a time of huge change in Southern Africa. The beginning of the end of colonial rule. A time of arrogance, elitism and delusion among the white Rhodesians. From as far back as I can remember, I was familiar with war and witness to the pain it brings. Television broadcasts started with the news at 5pm every day. This brought the latest developments in Vietnam into our living rooms, always followed by news of where fighting had occurred that day in our country, and how many people had been killed. This was followed by cartoons for the kids, a children's game show with "Cabby" or Batman and Robin. Nothing of this seemed abnormal to me, there was no insanity just life as usual. We learned nothing of the African culture, other than the white mans' interpretation of African history. A convenient justification for all things white, being right and good, no matter how it affected the locals. White Rhodesians justified their embattled independence by insisting the 'Rhodesian Black Man' had a better life style than any other 'Black Man' in Africa. Of course this openly discussed delusion continuously presented to the rest of the world only fanned the anger, rage, fury and hate of the Zimbabwean. At the time the population of Rhodesia consisted of

Live a Life That is Limitless

about 270 thousand European Africans/European Immigrants which was 7.2% of the total population of five million people.

Children brought their father's military reference booklets to school with photos of gun shot wounds. What heads look like when they have been shot once, twice or three times with 7.62 mm rounds. Pictures of how the human body decays in the African sun to help the security forces estimate time of death. Male school teachers spent their school holidays on compulsory service with their units fighting on the boarders. They returned unrested to the class room for the following term. I remember one man taking hold of my friend by his hair and smashing his head on the desk because he couldn't spell a word correctly. Brothers and fathers never came home. And those who did were never the same again.

When the British monitored the elections in 1980, the Rhodesian Secret Service estimated there were only seven thousand freedom fighters. Mugabe sent 17 thousand to hand in weapons, leaving an estimated 40 thousand strong army on the borders of Mozambique, just in case he didn't get the result he wanted. To put things into perspective, when I served as a Green Beret with the British forces there were seven thousand Royal Marine Commandos, and approximately 60 thousand ranks in the British Army. I guess if the Brits had intervened in anyway other than monitoring, I wouldn't be writing this.

Of course sexual abuse at such an early age creates immense confusion. Something so wrong being presented and encouraged as perfectly normal, with a hidden - can't put your finger on it - feeling that something isn't quite right. By the time I was ten years old, I'd had received extensive surgery on my hand, won all my swimming races, stopped wetting my bed and threatened to stab my abusers if they ever came near me again. Sounds intense and a life full of trauma and drama. That's where the delusional elitism of my Rhodesian psyche played an important part. I was after all a Rhodesian and no matter what shit happens to you, if you are a Rhodesian you will always win, even if you lose.
There was a popular song that every child sang at the time by Clem Tholet called 'Rhodesians Never Die".
The chorus went as follows:

Live a Life That is Limitless

"But we are all Rhodesians and we'll fight through thick and thin,
We'll keep our land a free land,
Stop the enemy coming in,
We'll keep them north of the Zambezi,
Until that river is running dry,
This mighty land will prosper,
For Rhodesians never die"

"Mmmm churr bro! Just as long as the dark green Rhodesians sit at the back of the bus so the light green Rhodesians can sit at the front!".

When I was 14 my parents emigrated to the UK. The culture shock was pretty intense. If it wasn't for my physical education teacher Mr. Peter Horne, I'm not sure where I would be today. He took me under his wing after noticing I was a strong swimmer and discovered I loved playing his two favourite sports. Most English kids don't usually play rugby and water polo, so he introduced me to the local rugby club and drove me 30 miles every week in the summer to train with his water polo team in Exmouth,

Devon. It was this journey that took us past the Commando Training Centre Royal Marines. Joining the forces was the last thing on my mind when I first arrived in the UK. At the time I thought it quite ironic that I had spent my whole childhood living in the middle of a war only to end up in a country that went to war three months after we arrived. My grand father had joined the Royal Marines in 1908 and served in both world wars, so I knew a bit about the organisation. I learned a lot more in 1982 when the UK Task forces were deployed to liberate Falkland Islanders from an Argentinian invasion. The conversations Peter and I had continued to spark my interest so I attempted to join up five months before my 16th birthday. I managed to pass the written exam before the careers officer noticed my age and promptly kick me out. I went back on the same day the following year and started my training 9 months later. I heard there were around 150 thousand applicants for the Royal Marines in 1984. Unemployment was high and the forces had become a popular choice after the success the British Forces had a couple of years previously in the Falkland Islands. That year the Royal Marines took about 600 new recruits. 21 young men showed up on the three day potential recruits selection

Live a Life That is Limitless

course I attended, three of us passed. I joined up with 47 men on the 24th September 1984. Thirteen men passed out as Commandos the following May.

In the spring of 1993 my unit returned home after a particularly mind numbing six month tour in Northern Ireland. We took a short spell of leave before redeploying to the Mediterranean. At the time I was an experienced Commando having completed two deployments (tours) to Northern Ireland and served in the Gulf. I was a military ski instructor having done 4 arctic tours and two leadership courses in the jungle. After being in Cyprus for a couple of weeks, a colleague and I decided to slip away from the barracks to explore the local area. We must have walked for quite a way when we came across a lone tavern on a back road in what appeared to be the middle of nowhere. While we enjoyed our meal a middle aged couple came in and were seated on the table next to us. They were very friendly and we could tell straight away he was a high ranking officer in the British forces. Probably a colonel or above. After we exchanged pleasantries about the weather and the fantastic food we were experiencing he asked us what we thought to be a strange question.

John Swanepoel

"What do you think we should do about Northern Ireland?"

His wife looked disinterested at this point. I said I had given it some consideration recently and had come up with two possible solutions. The first was relatively easy. We knew where the 200 or so IRA members lived. We could do a dawn synchronised kill of all of them. His wife rolled her eyes and carried on eating her lunch. He chuckled and nodded as if it was a reasonable idea under the current circumstances. I then continued to point out that choosing something like that was not only illegal, but would also end up making things far worse. I know if I was a kid and some soldiers had come to my home and executed my father I would be pretty angry. My anger, rage, fury and hate would be fuelled and everything would continue just as it had done for the past 24 years. He smiled and asked what my second option would be. I said we needed to start with the children. In my experience little children don't see other peoples colour or religion as something that is wrong or bad. This is taught to them by their parents and community. Most of the men in my unit

Live a Life That is Limitless

are of the opinion the British government have kept the conflict going so they have a live training ground for the forces. The terrorist groups keep going because they make huge amounts of money from the systems they have in place. Both sides then condition the general population through the media and politics to continue supporting their specific side. If we can find a way to integrate the young children from both sides in early learning centres and schools and show them a different way of being things would start to change. Of course this is a gross simplification of a process that in reality would take a couple of generations. His wife started taking notice with a huge smile on her face. She nodded and looked surprised. He shook his head and looked a little disappointed. I guess that was the time I finally realised the futility and senselessness of war. Where the only winner is the organisation making the equipment, weapons and ammunition.

When I finally left the forces after 11.5 years service I struggled with manic depression with Bipolar tendencies, although I would never have put myself in a position where I could have been diagnosed with anything like that. I had come from an elite organisation after being brought up in a delusionally elitist environment. Depression and Bipolar behaviour was for lesser individuals. Sign of weakness!! Harden up man you are the best of the best, Bootnecks don't get depressed, we are trained to maintain a sense of humour in adversity, one of the most important characteristics of a Commando. I should note that this is not how the Royal Marines operate, I was just insane. In the Corps, if a man has a problem he is helped immediately. The difficulty is getting the man to admit he has a problem. Most men keep their mouths shut until they leave the job. The Commando spirit creates a unique bond not to be underestimated. Bootnecks use their awesome sense of humour to comfort and support one another, and it is one of the most endearing qualities of the brotherhood I dearly miss.

My insanity also created the point of view that my physiotherapy degree, although pretty intense, was not hard enough. So I took a job working 48 hours a week doing 12 hour night shifts in nursing homes even though I had enough money to see me through my degree. This was the darkest period in my life as I came to realise later. It is

Live a Life That is Limitless

only once you have healed that you realise how ill you actually were.

In 2001 I met my partner who was about to emigrate to New Zealand with her daughter. I had to make the decision of letting her go or following her to the other side of the world. As I mentioned earlier, I didn't know much about New Zealand so I kept it simple. They love rugby and speak English, so what's not to like? In 2002 I emigrated to New Zealand and my partner and I started our own practice. In 2004 our physiotherapy company had reached full capacity by the end of the first year of trading. We were looking to expand and were considering creating a high end centre for neurological rehabilitation. One of our tetraplegic patients kept hounding us to approach his father who owned some undeveloped land in the industrial area of Mt Maunganui. After some consideration I set up a meeting to discuss the possibility of creating a custom built centre. Of course ego dictated it was to be the best private facility in the country. I designed the building and sourced all the equipment. My partner and I invested our life savings into the business. We created a gym, cafe and specialist treatment facility.

Dame Susan Devoy opened the doors on 15th October 2005, two months after my daughter was born. By the end of 2008 we were in the black and able to expand again. I had designed the building so this could be done easily. In 2009 we added six specialised treatment rooms, and a conference centre. We ran the largest elderly care contract in the country and things were looking great, until the government changed. Everything dried up. No more referrals, contracts were put on hold unofficially, and stalling tactics were used by the new government for all physiotherapy contracts. The situation was serious. We had to down size immediately. We were struggling to pay the rent and needed to close the doors or we would lose everything. Of course the landlord - a multi millionaire who owns a well known fuel distribution company - insisted we stay open. He reassured us that he would support us as he said what we were doing was very important for the community. He regularly said "Just call me Santa Claus, pay me what you can afford I'll sort the rest". Fifteen months later he told us we owed him the difference on the 15 months rent we had not been able to cover and told us we had to give him all of our equipment. When I told him that wasn't going to happen he waited

Live a Life That is Limitless

until we closed one Friday evening and changed the locks. We went to open up on the Saturday and of course couldn't get in. He left his tetraplegic son in his wheel chair to man the door and let us know we could not return until we agreed to give him all of the equipment. On Saturday afternoon I made some calls. There are ex Royal Marines all over the world, and the average Kiwi is the most loyal individual on the planet. With the help of an ex patient who owns a delivery company and some close mates we cleared the building between 6am and 11am that Sunday. My gym manager txt me the same afternoon and said he had been called into the centre by the stunned landlord, who had turned up to gloat over his recently illegally acquired hoard only to find an empty building. Seeing his face that afternoon would have been a small consolation. We had lost everything and more importantly, the people we were there to help, had nowhere else to go. Over the coming 12 months we sold off the equipment and paid all outstanding bills. The landlord turned out to be a lier, thief and wilfully deceitful individual. We had signed the lease and had no written proof or recorded proof of the conversations I had with the landlord over previous 18 months. We had a good working relationship, I had not thought it necessary to have him put anything in writing. A mistake I will never make again. He continued to pursue us through the High Court just because he could, so my partner and I chose to file for bankruptcy in 2012 which has turned out to be the best thing that could have happened.

Since then I have spent everyday with my children, taking them to and from school. Until then I had been working huge hours in the business fighting to keep everything. It has been a privilege to watch them grow up without the prejudices I experienced at their age and being able to support them in all of their activities. We were able to take a breath and explore parts of New Zealand we hadn't see yet. I was able to continue my studies in Alternative Medicine and Access Consciousness, wrote books and took workshops. I travelled overseas to complete my post graduate level studies in the PaRama Bodytalk System, and continued treating my patients in my clinic at home.

It has been a humbling experience recognising how the small abused child became an angry bully and how those aspects of my childhood were reflected in the subtle

Live a Life That is Limitless

abuses I experienced and allowed for so long in my own relationship. The more profound learning came from the understanding I gained of how the military conditioning makes it so difficult for service personal to recover from PTSD, and how effective the Bodytalk System is for this problem. In 2005 I recognised the Bodytalk System as an effective alternative health modality and became a practitioner. In 2007 I met up with a close friend and colleague for an infrequent Bodytalk swop session. The single session turned into three over a couple of weeks and I have not suffered from depression since. I stepped out of the insanity into the awareness of the state I had been in all of my life. It took a PaRama Bodytalk session with the founder of the system Dr. John Veltheim some five years later to finally unravel the military conditioning that released the anger, rage fury and hate I was holding.

The Personal Focus System is an advanced personal development course which has been created off the back of my life experiences and learning. This book is the reference material for the workshops I run teaching practical application of everything that is presented here.

THE FIRST ANALOGY.

What if, somewhere way back in history a small group of individuals had an idea. Maybe those 'wise' fellows noticed, that humans tended to keep things simple. They noticed the harder the penis the bigger the reward and decided it would be an excellent idea to convince everyone else this profound observation should be applied to everything else in their lives. The universal law of "The harder something is the better". It must be true they thought. The hard penis creates beautiful new things and feels great. So people began to believe the harder life was the greater their reward would be. Then just in case they didn't get an amazing reward for all their hard work in this life, they decided they had better include an assurance that they would definitely get an even greater reward in the next life.

Live a Life That is Limitless

Could this be the insanity which has been passed on through generations, resulting in humanity being manipulated, vulnerable and abused on a global scale. The vulnerability of mankind lies in the ease with which an individual can be manipulated through anger, guilt, fear, money, sex and business. The reactions these cause, create the emotional triggers that are used to manipulate and control the masses. It locks people in reaction, keeping them fully distracted through the trauma and drama whipped up around them. Fear of not having enough, not being good enough, fear of loosing everything or being wrong. Whipping the masses into a frenzy and convincing them the best way out with the biggest rewards is hard work. The harder everything is the bigger the reward.

"Not true! the ONLY thing that should be hard in life is a penis!"

It is time for humanity to wake up and see the limitations of our conditioning for what they are. Once we become aware of the ways we have been conditioned that are limiting us, we can choose something different. Once we choose to stop reacting to the fear, anger and guilt we can no longer be distracted from creating fulfilling lives from a place of total ease.

This book is an opportunity to tap into aspects of Self you may not have considered possible. By choosing to investigate how visualisation can be used to enhance your life, you have started on a journey that will undoubtedly shift your self awareness, increase your consciousness of self worth and actualise a life beyond your wildest dreams.

This book is for people who are willing to develop techniques that up until recent times would have been considered mumbo jumbo. There will be generalised explanations of our mind and how it functions. I will introduce you to alternative ways of recognising the belief systems you have aligned yourself to that may be hindering you from achieving your full potential. You will be given tools that enhance your awareness of the choices you are making that are not working for you, and will show you how to use the tools to help you choose what does work for you.

Live a Life That is Limitless

For millennia mankind has understood the power of visualisation. In many cases this knowledge has been hidden from humanity by the few who were aware of our unlimited potential as infinite beings. All known ancient civilisations have recognised the Pineal as the visual centre. The symbol used has been the pine cone which can be found depicted through all major religions in the world and all ancient civilisations. I will not be presenting or discussing the evidence of this in any detail as I'd rather stay on track with teaching you how to develop your visualisation skills. There are other authors who give excellent scientific summations of the research and observations that confirm these facts.

We have been manipulated over many years to believe happiness and security can be gained through hard work. Do as you are told and give the right answers and you can achieve anything. The idea that happiness is earned through hard work is a untruth. You are more likely to reap tiredness, bitterness and resentment through hard work.

This book will give you the tools to dissolve the conditioning you have received that continues to limit you. You will be shown how much fun you can have when you tap into your full potential, without falling into the manipulation of belief systems and other peoples points of view, which create the foundations of your conditioning and subconsciously self-imposed limitations. Then you can start creating a life of total ease that is a truth for you, fulfilling, rewarding and full of fun.

CHAPTER ONE

THE BODY CONSOLE IN THE MAINFRAME.

The system you will learn here has been used for millennia. Acknowledged by every know civilisation. It has remained hidden in plain sight from every human being. You will learn how to use this powerful system to your advantage and which toxins have been introduced to our societies that suppress our ability to use the system with

Live a Life That is Limitless

ease.

The human race has continued to buy into the distractions around us which are continuing to limit our ability to create a life of total ease and fun. I will show you just how limiting the distractions we choose to buy into can be, and how to recognise the distractions for what they are. Once you have grasped this analogy and have a good understanding of the rest of Part One of this book, you will be able to apply what you have learned to the visualisation systems taught in Part Two. Read Part One of this book at least three times before starting the practical application process in Part Two. And above all, have fun.

Your body can be likened to a carbon based highly complex game console functioning within the mainframe of collective consciousness. What does this mean? It means that in order for every human game console to be part of the game of 'Life on Earth' we need a convincing and realistic console in a realistic playing environment. Science has
long acknowledged we are only energy. Everything in our world is made up of energy and everything has its own

unique recipe of energy.

Albert Einstein once said.
" Everything is energy and that's all there is to it. Match the frequency of the reality you want and you cannot help but get that reality. It can be no other way. This is not philosophy. This is physics"

I like to visualise each individual recipe as a multi dimensional template that has a unique vibration or frequency. The template is the foundation for the manifestation of our bodies and every other physical and energetic construct in the universe.This vibration of consciousness is created from the quantum particulates that create everything, from all known Elements, to the DNA that pulses through every part of the universe. A vibration of consciousness that is governed by the universal laws. The energetic template holds the information that eventually actualises physically. Every energetic template is unique and is what creates the diversity we experience through our lives.

It is the collective consciousness that creates the main-

Live a Life That is Limitless

frame. The mainframe provides a physical foundation that enables our 'Game Consoles" to build cities, recognise hills and mountains, design and build our own homes, recognise all other living consoles plants and animals. It is the mainframe that gives each one of us the platform from which the context of our reality is created and maintained. The back drop to support the stories surrounding our everyday extra ordinary lives.

To begin with I will show you what I ask everyone I work with. I use this analogy to create awareness of how distracted we are through our lives.

CHAPTER TWO

THE CONVERSATION ...

I will give the answers that are given 90% of the time. Anna's would be the standard answers I get during this conversation.

John: Anna, do you have a Soul?
Anna: Yup ....
John: Does it ever die?
Anna: Not sure, guess so ....
John: Truth ... Does it ever die?
Anna: No
John: Ah .... so you are an infinite being?
Anna: Guess so yup.

John: OK Good......Hold your hand in front of your face ....

Live a Life That is Limitless

Anna lifts her hand in front of her face and looks at it.

John: Is that you?

Anna: Yes ....

John: How can that be you? You have just said you are infinite ....

Anna: Ah ... no thats my body.

John: Ok Good. So we don't know who 'YOU' are. 'YOU' is an infinite being playing in Anna Game Console. Anna is a living being, a complex organic game console, 'YOU' gets to experience. This is the only way 'YOU' gets to feel the intensity of the different emotions Anna experiences everyday. 'YOU' brings the power of the Infinite to Anna Console and integrates that power into Anna. Anna is a high powered organic console, custom built to fit and integrate 'YOU' perfectly. So 'YOU' becomes an integral part of Anna.

Anna: Hmmm I hadn't thought of it that way before.

John: Lets consider the Anna Game Console. She is an amazing complex creation that constantly loves and supports 'YOU' from the moment she was born to the moment she chooses to die. Anna Console is constantly processing all the emotional traumas and dramas she experiences. She has a complex motherboard that is standard issue throughout the human race. It has a number of Apps built into it specifically designed to distract Anna from YOU.

Anna: Why does Anna need to be distracted from the 'YOU'?

John: Good question ... Would an infinite being ever be without too much money, perfect health or perfect relationships?

Anna: I wouldn't have thought an infinite being would need any of those things.

John: OK ... So the Infinite Being "YOU", only knows total allowance. Unconditional love, no good or bad right or

Live a Life That is Limitless

wrong. The Infinite Being is the part of the self that is God consciousness, a little piece of God, the link to or part of The Source Field, The Zero Point, The Super Conscious State, Pure Energy, or The Field, which ever you prefer. The place where there can be no reaction, no trauma or drama only total allowance in everything. We just agreed that as an infinite being 'YOU' already knows everything there is to know. 'YOU' can create anything at anytime. Too much money, a body with perfect health that never ages, perfect abundant relationships. If everything was totally perfect all the time what would 'YOU' do? 'YOU' already knows total allowance and unconditional love. How would 'YOU' amuse 'YOURSELF'? Who would understand 'YOU'? Who would even like to spend time with 'YOU' if there was no trauma and drama?

... John Smiles

Anna: Ok ... so the Apps are there to keep the Anna Console busy so she doesn't use the 'YOU' too much?

John: Yes nice one ..... Yes ...... Lets call the Apps 'Reactor Apps'. When a Reactor App is tapped all that can happen is Anna Console goes into Total Distraction from the YOU.

Anna: So what would be a Reactor App?

John: There are many which I will cover in more detail later. Have you ever been blamed for something you did not do?

Anna: Yes many times.

John: So how did that make you feel?

Anna: Angry I guess, and frustrated.

John: So Anna Console's "Blame Reactor App" was pushed . It was the Lie of being blamed for something she didn't do that also tapped her Anger App which made her release the Anger neuropeptide that made her feel angry. Anna Consoles frustration was from the lack of information she had about why someone would blame her for something she did not do. The moment the "Blame and Anger Reactor Apps" were tapped Anna Console was launched into Distraction from "YOU" and

Live a Life That is Limitless

so plays out the Distraction for as long as it takes.

"YOU" gets to enjoy the experience of anger and frustration.

Anna: So a Lie will always make you angry and Frustration is always just a lack of information.

John: Yup, Exactly right….

Anna: So how do I stop feelings of anger and frustration?

John: Let's say 'YOU' has 100% (Infinite) capacity available to contribute while playing in the Anna Console. On a good day, Anna Console probably only uses 1% of the 100%, because she is constantly distracted from her full potential by the emotional states generated by all the Reactor Apps that are running. Each emotion has its own special group of recipes called emotional neuropeptides. These emotional neuropeptides are produced in the part of the brain called the hypothalamus, and when released into the blood stream, makes us feel a specific way. There are six categories of emotion: Joy/Sadness, Worry,

Grief, Fear and Anger. Each category has a number of different recipes which all produce a slightly different feeling. Feelings are always just a feeling and nothing else. Our feelings create the intensity of every experience we have. They are the fuel that drives how we react. The belief systems and interesting thoughts we align ourselves to are the foundations for the choices we make.

Anna: So when a Reactor App is pushed the distraction we go into is as a result of us feeling a certain way..... Like feeling Pissed Off because your mum won't let you stay overnight at your best mates party?

John: Yup ....

Anna: But it's the beliefs I have about how I'm mature and responsible enough to stay overnight that are causing me to be pissed off and angry in the first place.

John: You got it. Our beliefs determine how much of a Distraction we will go into. Dissolve the beliefs and points of view you have aligned yourself too and your Reactor Apps

Live a Life That is Limitless

will stop working for that particular story.

Anna: How do I do that ... how do I dissolve or even know which beliefs are causing me to go into reaction?

John: Good question .... Anna Console has another very important built in function that is her 'Get Out of Distraction Switch'.

Notice I said, 'Get out of Distraction NOT 'Get out of Reaction' More on that later.

The 'Get Out of Distraction Switch' is called Awareness. Let's call it the 'A Switch'. The 'A Switch' can be flipped anytime she chooses once she becomes aware it exists. Once she has the awareness an 'A' Switch exists, she will start to notice when a Reactor App has been tapped and recognise the belief system attached to that App. This is when she can start to dissolve the belief system so she never reacts to that story again. Only then can she begin to tap into the remaining 99% she truly be.

Anna: So why don't we just know this already? If 'YOU' knows everything there is to know, how does Anna get to use that knowledge?

John: 'YOU' knows EVERYTHING ...... Anna Console is just not AWARE of EVERYTHING. Her brain doesn't have the capacity to hold all of that information at once. However, she can access any part of the EVERYTHING by simply asking questions....

The paradigm of the "YOU" and the Body Console.

YOU = total allowance and unconditional love.

Body Console = emotional reaction and feelings.

YOU is here to experience what emotion feels like through creating trauma and drama with the help of the Body Console and the Reactor Apps.

Body Console is trying to achieve peace and calm and understand total allowance.

Live a Life That is Limitless

YOU gets to experience the human experience.

Body Console learns to overcome the drama and trauma created by the reactions it goes into when it has its belief systems challenged.

CHAPTER THREE

The Limitations of Our Beliefs.

Our beliefs help us create the choices we make. Belief systems have been established through our environment and the society we live in. The foundation beliefs our parents hold will have been handed down through generations. When we sit and really think about beliefs and where they originate from, no-one really knows how old they are or where they come from. All beliefs are created from Judgement. Judging something to be right or wrong, good or bad, creates the foundation for the beliefs we take on.

Judgment is a limitation.

To be in judgement we have to have come to a series of conclusions. Conclusion by definition is an end. It means we can go no further. This locks us into the judgement, which becomes the foundations of a belief.

To judge something to be right or good we have to align and agree with a point of view. Once we do this we tend to defend that point of view. We will do anything to keep it Right which includes aligning ourselves to any other points of view that will support the original judgement. The opposite happens when we resist or react to a point of view. This is when we judge a point of view to be Wrong or Bad.

Aligning and Agreeing (Making Right)
When we align and agree with a point of view, we ignore any limitations that point of view creates for us because we have made it right.

Resisting and Reacting (Making Wrong)
When we resist and react to a point of view, we ignore any possibilities that point of view could create for us because we have made it wrong.

This is one of the foundations behind the fear, anger, rage, fury and hate we see all around us today. People using personal beliefs as a foundation to justify their anger, rage, fury and hate towards others.

An Inuit Indian in Northern Canada will never see the world in the same way as an Eban in the jungles of Brunei. Their worlds are too different. Although their game consoles are made the same way with the same Reactor Apps, their beliefs will differ because the part of the mainframe they are playing in is totally different and presents totally different challenges. The Inuit and the Eban are examples of extremes in climate and culture, no different to the diversities in beliefs and cultures within our communities today.

No matter where we are in the world, there are communities who are split by cultural differences and beliefs: some living right next door to one another. We have all been born humans. We have the same consoles with the same Reactor Apps. We are all connected energetically in the mainframe of collective consciousness. It's the beliefs we have been conditioned into that are tapping the

Reactor Apps of Fear, Anger, Guilt, Shame, Blame, Hate and Fury. How would our world be if we were aware every

Live a Life That is Limitless

time something or someone tapped one of our Reactor Apps and set our body console off into reaction. We would see the Reactions for what they are.

CHAPTER FOUR

"And It's Right" Reactor App

Not so long ago I was watching an Australian TV documentary. The presenter was interviewing a young Muslim mother. The young woman was in her early 20's in a happy stable relationship. She told her personal story in detail answering all the questions the reporter asked her calmly and with dignity. As she walked down her local high street passersby shouted insults at her and her young children.

She told how she was brought up in a strict Muslim family and how she drifted away from the faith while a teenager. When she met her husband she returned to the faith. She explained how happy and content she was following the faith. She mentioned how strong her relationship was

Live a Life That is Limitless

with her husband, how supportive and loving he was of her. How she wears her burka with pride and hasn't been as happy in her life as she was at that moment. She finished by saying.

"And it's Right!"

I observed with a smile as it was clearly something that was working really well for both her and her husband. She was happy, content and supported by her husband. Her choices were working really well for her. A TRUTH for them both: something that felt light and filled them both with joy.

I was brought up in a Christian home. My mother was a minister in a Christian church and had been sent to Africa as a missionary where she met my father. I was expected to attend Sunday school every week, take part in the children's choir and

play in the brass band. All for Jesus, to save the sinners because it was right.

Both my parents were unaware I was being sexually, emotionally and psychologically abused between the ages of three and ten. In my experience the hypocrisy continued when we emigrated to the UK. The teens in the English church, after promising to refrain from drinking alcohol, smoking cigarettes and taking drugs, used to spend some of their Sunday mornings having a quick puff in the back alley followed by the occasional swig of beer. One of the choir singers who was seven years my senior, much to my delight, had decided to pop my cherry. She continued to take good care of me every Sunday afternoon, returning to sing in the choir every Sunday evening as if butter wouldn't melt in her mouth. A teenage boy's dreams come true.

I was then expected to continue my ministry for Jesus by playing in the band and attending services regularly. By 15 years of age there was just too much hypocrisy for me to continue. I wasn't there for the Right reasons. So I sacrificed my Sunday afternoon copulation and refused to go to church. I was then punished through guilt and no money. My mother used emotional abuse to try and ma-

Live a Life That is Limitless

nipulate me back to church. She cried regularly insisting this was not how I was brought up. My father supported her by refusing to continue giving me pocket money.

When I left School a year later, I took a part time job in a supermarket stacking shelves and started a pre services course at the local college. This continued until I started Commando Training with the British Forces one year later.

While serving in the first Gulf war there were many Muslim men who shared a beer with my colleagues and I during Ramadan, in both the UAE and Bahrain. I understand those who follow the Muslim faith refrain from drinking alcohol and honour the fasting period of Ramadan. These men presented themselves as Muslim yet chose to ignore the rules of the faith they where born into. I personally have no point of view either way. This is just human nature. Every man makes his choices for whatever reason and that is his business.

I was born into a Christian family, which I also consider to be irrelevant. Whether you believe Jesus is the son of God or a lowly prophet is up to you. I understand his messages were always offered in total allowance (Unconditional Love). I believe all religions started from a single source. This would explain why there are many messages that are consistent through all religions.

The "And its right!" is the global trigger that gets pulled every day. The limitation we impose on ourselves. The button that is being pushed in every
nation, region, community and individual: like a giant international reactor app.

There are estimated to be 38640 different sects of Christianity in the world today (David Wilcox, The Source Field Investigations), each with their own Interesting Thoughts (I.T.'s) of how one should worship. Every major religion in the world has sects. Each sect believes they are Right. As I'm certain every religion has hypocrisy, rumbling in the back ground. It's human nature.

What if we could read all religious text from a place of total allowance? How would the respective texts read if we could see every message is given from unconditional love and total allowance. What if Spirit has no fear anger or rage. No hate, right or wrong, good or bad, only total

Live a Life That is Limitless

allowance. True and False are judgements and therefore limitations imposed by belief systems created from Judgement.

Truth is a universal law. That just means Truth can never be hidden. All major religions have the same messages within their texts. Find the messages they all have in common and you find the Truth.

"Love Thy Neighbour " is misunderstood. Love is a judgement. The misunderstanding is in how each person in the world understands what love is. No one really has a clue what you are talking about when you say something like "I love you". How can they, they haven't lived your life, they have no clue how you see the world.

A couple of years ago there was a local court case. The man on trial had beaten his girl friend up and thrown her in the boot of his car. When he drove off she climbed out but unfortunately her leg got stuck and she was dragged along the ground. She was seriously injured and lost her leg as a result. The court asked the man why he had done this to his girlfriend. He said it was because he loved her.

He was found guilty and locked up for a long time. Even if he did love her, we don't know what love meant to him. He may have been beaten and locked in a cupboard every time he did

something wrong as a kid. Then told he was loved when his parents dragged him out the next day. That would make beating his girl friend acceptable to him. Or he may have just been trying to limit his time in prison.

This is not just relevant for Religion. I have used Religion as an example as it is the foundation behind all wars. Its is used by those who wish to manipulate the masses to make obscene amounts of money. A continued manipulation of humanity to line their pockets by supplying both sides with the ammunition to continue the fight, as has been done through all modern wars. And it is easy for them to continue as long as we are willing to keep making each other wrong. And fighting to stay Right.

This "And Its Right" is used in every society at every level. From inter-school competitions to national and international politics. Reasons for perpetuating misery in

Live a Life That is Limitless

the world through our conditioning, which always ends with both sides being affected by loss. Meanwhile the people at the top grow richer and more motivated to create new ways of creating more wealth using the same Reactor Apps.

A 5.56mm round is the standard calibre round used by most of the western forces today. A single round costs $0.50. Anti personal bombs and rockets vary between $60,000 and $600,000.00+ for a single round. How may rounds are fired everyday in the world? A great big cha ching!!!! with every shot. Your hard earned cash, the tax payers money lining the pockets of the 1% who own everything. These are not the politicians as we are lead to believe. The politicians are the puppets at the top of the pile of distracted humans we have been conditioned into.

George Carlin Says.
"Military cemeteries around the world are packed with brainwashed dead soldiers who were convinced God was on their side. America prays for God to destroy our enemies. Our enemies pray for God to destroy us. Some-

body's gonna be disappointed. Somebody's wasting their fucking time.
Could it be...... Everyone?"

It is the fear that has been cleverly engineered through all societies that creates the foundation for the "And Its Right" Reactor Apps. Once the foundation is set using the belief systems of the region, the people who are manipulating us can get to work tapping Reactor Apps. Ask yourself how many times have you had your "And Its Right" Reactor App tapped in the past week. What stories are being spun in the media this week about terror around the world and how we justify the fight against it.

As with the young Muslim family in the documentary, they were harming no one yet they were being abused while they walked along the pavement in their home town. Yet they were happy with the choices they made around how they live their lives.

We all need to learn acceptance. Put the fear, resentment, anger, blame, rage, shame, and fury behind us. Its what makes a very few people obscene amounts of money, and

Live a Life That is Limitless

causes the rest of humanity untold pain and suffering on a global scale.

This manipulation of humanity could be stopped today as soon as we choose to acknowledge there will always be differences in the way people choose to live. The differences we see every day that make people happy are a Truth for them. Our Truth makes us happy but isn't necessarily Light for everyone else. Accepting one another for who we are and being in total allowance of one another will change the pile of distracted disconnected humans into a power house of humanity no longer be manipulated through their conditioning.

So once we achieve the bed of roses how do we deal with the thorns?

Let's keep it simple. If a group of people are choosing to move into a community that has a different culture they should be in allowance of that culture and abide by the cultural laws to a point where they don't compromise their own truth. If they are unable to achieve this with total ease, this way of life is a Lie for them. They should find a community where they can reside without conflict, in total allowance of one another and acknowledge the other communities are living their truth and that is OK. To those who feel the need to impose their beliefs and way of life onto others, I ask -

And you would limit yourself by judging someone else to be wrong for what reason? - Live peacefully in your Truth and allow others to do the same, you are dearly loved -

CHAPTER FIVE

Making Ourselves Wrong

When we look back to the first conversation and we remind ourselves of the analogy of the YOU and Anna Game console we can create another perspective. Anna Console is an organic carbon based life form with physical and emotional needs. YOU has the privilege of playing

Live a Life That is Limitless

through Anna Console to experience all the things YOU can't experience without a body. So Anna is the only

living being that will love and support "YOU" from the moment she was created to the moment she chooses to die. Anna is influenced by the belief systems, and other peoples points of view she has, which YOU uses to continuously criticise and judge her to be right or wrong, good or bad.

Self judgment is the harshest limitation we can impose on ourselves. Judging ourselves to be "Not Good Enough" creates a series of limiting beliefs. Every day we stand in front of the mirror and judge ourselves. Too fat, too thin, not fit enough, bum looks too big in this, too many spots, need a hair cut and anything else you can think of that you tell yourself every day. These are judgments we impose on ourselves because of the belief systems we have aligned and agreed with or resisted and reacted to. This then creates the belief that people can see us the way we see ourselves. The limitations start coming as we walk out the door. We've undermined our own confidence by judging ourselves to be wrong in some way. We then project that judgement into our world which attracts judgement of us through our projections. That's why people always notice the things about you, you really don't want them too.

What would your world look like if you could be in total allowance of yourself and the people around you?

No more judgement, no more ridicule, no more abuse.

Would your game suddenly stop?

Would your body disintegrate or burst into flames?

Or would you catch a glimpse of what unconditional love, joy and ease looks and feels like?

Once we no longer judge our Body Consoles to be faulty we create the space and the ability to be vulnerable enough to allow ourselves to be totally judged by everyone and anyone we meet. Once you allow yourself to be totally judged … you can't be…. and the distraction created from the emotional reactions you have been locked into will disappear.

CHAPTER SIX

Sensing what is Light or Heavy

Instead of making things right or wrong and good or bad. Use Light or Heavy. This is not an exercise in semantics as many will assume at first glance. The right and wrong, good and bad are from the limitations of the conclusions we have come to about specific Interesting Thoughts. These conclusions form the foundations of the beliefs we align and agree with or resist and react to and will always have Reactor Apps attached to them.

The Reactor App is there to create feelings that heighten our physiological experience. When a Reactor App is tapped, it creates the feelings we experience like happiness, sadness, anger, worry, grief and fear.

When you choose to use light or heavy to describe a situation, we are using our subtle senses to create awareness if something is going to create ease or difficulty in our world. There is no feeling associated with choosing Light or Heavy as they are not aligned with any Interesting Thoughts or Belief Systems.

Choosing from a place that you sense is Light will always create results faster than you could ever expect. When a choice feels light to you it will make you smile and your body will buzz and respond with ease. When you sense something to be light for you it will be a Truth for you.

Truth is a Universal Law. It is recognised through all civilisations that the Truth can never be hidden. When we say "TRUTH" before asking a question there can be no lies. Try asking a young child of three or four if they have done something you know they have, which they know they should not have. Ask "Truth, did you paint this picture on the wall?" Their answer will usually be "Yes NO!".

With adults and older children, understanding the body language that accompanies a lie will bring confirmation. A

Live a Life That is Limitless

person cannot lie with Truth. Most people just pause for a second and then tell the truth anyway.

When you choose something that you sense is HEAVY it is usually a lie. When we choose HEAVY, results happen far slower, usually with barriers, the enjoyment tends to be lost and everything turns into a high stressed grind. We have a tendency to over rationalise which sticks us and chokes the flow through over analysis. We go into negative reaction which is unhappiness and depressive states and think there is something wrong with us. Maybe there is nothing wrong with you. Maybe you just chose something which is a lie for you and your body.

CHAPTER SEVEN

Everything Is Just An "Interesting Thought"

When we choose from judgment we are always in reaction. Reaction is the emotional response we create that perpetuates how we feel and enables psychologists to predict how we might behave or react in a given situation. Psychologists have studied human behaviour and how the brain works for years. They are able to identify specific personality traits and predict how a person is likely to react under certain circumstances. When we learn to recognise that everything is just an "interesting thought" (IT) we are able to stop aligning and agreeing or resisting and reacting to interesting thoughts and beliefs systems that are holding us in a perpetual state of reaction.

Live a Life That is Limitless

If we can change the language we use we can start to create possibilities we would have never considered. By avoiding using Right or Wrong and Good or Bad we can start to tap into our right brain and use the felt sense which is far more powerful. Our true power comes from a place where there is no reaction only Observation. When we are Observing something, we can create far more mental and physical clarity. Developing the Right brain is to develop the ability to sense rather than feel.

CHAPTER EIGHT

Observing

Observing is when we have flicked the 'A' Switch (Awareness Switch) and are no longer distracted by a story. This is the time we are calm and un-opinionated about the story unfolding before us. A place where we recognise how we aligned ourselves to a beliefs system or interesting thought

that created the story. We begin to no longer align ourselves to those beliefs and interesting thoughts we had about the story. Once you have flicked the "A" Switch the reactions we experience become less intense. The longer you keep the awareness the 'A' switch creates, the sooner you lose the need to hold the belief system that caused the reaction in the first place.

Live a Life That is Limitless

Once we are Observing we start to interact with everyone around us from a place of No Judgment. We no longer hook into the self-judgement projections people are making about themselves. So we stop judging people from their projections. This is when you can literally say anything and there will be no reaction. A person can only react when they are judged and are not Observing.

This is the moment when everything literally becomes an Interesting Thought (IT). The moment you can see everything is just an 'Interesting Thought' is the moment you have cleared a path through the dense jungle of your belief systems. The more often you flick the 'A' Switch the wider the path becomes. Once you have created a motorway through the jungle of your beliefs you have built the foundation to begin living from awareness and observation. This is 'THE NOW', the most powerful place we create our lives from. The 'Now', is the Moment we can become the Question and the Choice, not the Reaction and Distraction.

With Awareness and Observation we are able to keep ourselves from the Distraction, that is created from the

Reactions we experience when, the Beliefs and Interesting Thoughts we hold are challenged.

CHAPTER NINE

The "A" Switch and the Peptaholic.

So you get to the point where you start using the "A" switch. You start recognising all the interesting points of view people have. You start listening into conversations and hearing all the stories people are playing out. You recognise the roles they are playing, and start to recognise which reactor Apps

have been tapped. You start to understand IT and recognise the different belief systems people are bringing with them or buying into.

All this isn't going to stop your Reactor Apps from being tapped. They are far too strong and embedded in your

Live a Life That is Limitless

"Body Console". Remember they are standard issue. Plugged into your mother board like USB pen drives as if each Reactor App has its own software programme assigned to it.

When a Reactor App is tapped is when the reaction begins. Each App has a number of peptide recipes in its software programme that create an emotional response. Your emotions make the story feel real.

This is the perfect time to flick the "A" Switch, pause a moment and allow yourself to recognise you are just experiencing what a peptide feels like. You will begin to recognise those Beliefs and Interesting Thoughts (IT's) you hold that created the story in the first place and you will STILL react to the emotional hit you have just experienced from having a particular Reactor App activated. You can't help it. The peptide is too strong, like a hit from a class A drug.

As the peptide enters your blood stream the feeling kicks in and the emotion will surge through your system. Your 'Body Console' will have to process it gradually dissipating the peptide until the feeling goes. Sometimes you then look to reinforce and repeat the hit. Like a junky injecting himself again and again.

This is when you start repeating the story. By repeating the story you are setting yourself up to create another surge of emotion. You will choose the group, friend or family member who you know will sympathise with your story. As you repeat the story you repeat the peptide hit. You feel the emotional surge again and so the reaction and distraction continues. Round in circles - like you don't have a choice - until that game no longer works for you.

Flicking the "A" Switch allows us to see a reaction for what it is, "A perfect distraction from our full potential". Once we have the awareness that we are in distraction we can start to appreciate the power of the peptide and the amazing intensity of emotion a chemical recipe has given us.

Even though you are feeling the emotion, this is the moment you are able to Observe how you feel without being thrown into distraction.

Live a Life That is Limitless

Feeling the emotion without becoming distracted by it, enables you to clearly see the Interesting

Thought for what it is. Just an IT. Everyone is entitled to an IT and that after all is only what it is.

 A number of years ago when my children were very young my partner and I were in business together. We ran a rehab centre specialising in neurological rehabilitation for people recovering from spinal injuries, head injuries and stroke. At the time I had only been practicing and integrating the Bodytalk System with my Physical Therapy and Acupuncture practice for a couple of years. The Bodytalk System is probably best described as integrated consciousness medicine. Practitioners learn how the different parts of the body have a responsibility to help process consciousness and the emotions. These concepts and interesting
thoughts have been observed for thousands of years in Traditional Chinese Medicine and the Ayurvedic medical systems and in more recent times within Chiropractic consciousness studies.

On this particular day I received an urgent call from my partner to say she was held up and needed me to organise transport and accommodation for a specialist she was flying over from South

Africa. I asked her for the details of his flights and where he would be conducting his courses and promptly started organising everything for her. An hour later I texted her saying "no worries job done", to which she replied with a phone call. She asked me what I had done and when I told her I had organised everything she had asked for, she then proceeded to tell me all the information she had left out during our first conversation, and that our practice manager had already organised everything so I'd better cancel my arrangements because I had got everything wrong.

Of course my Anger App was tapped and I went off into the distraction of anger. I wasn't aware of my 'A' switch in those days. I didn't have anyone to communicate with. Our practice manager had done an awesome job. I wouldn't see my partner until the evening. So I continued

Live a Life That is Limitless

working while my anger festered. I had wasted an hour of my precious time coordinating something I didn't have all the information for, while our practice manager wasted our companies time organising something for our regional physiotherapy board.

At the end of the day I picked my two children up from their carer. When I dropped them off that morning I had promised we would stop for ice cream on our way home. While driving to the ice cream parlour my lower back went into spasm. I could barely get out of the car and had to refuse my little girl when she asked me to pick her up. I sat uncomfortably while my kids enjoyed their ice cream. I knew exactly where the spasm was taking place, I knew what to do to ease it. I went home and cooked dinner in between stretches and when my partner returned home she instantly knew to maintain a wide berth.

My spasm was at L5/S1. I was angry because I had not been able to communicate my frustration at having my time wasted during the day. L5/S1 helps to process the consciousness of anger, difficulty in communicating and inability to accept pleasure. The pain was an exquisite

8/10, and as I struggled with the dinner I realised I liked it. I liked the fact I was angry it was like a high, and I didn't want anyone to take the moment away from me. In my eyes it was fully justified. A disregard for my personal time and a disregard for my efforts that I was unable to defend at the moment I needed to. I went to bed early and continued to wake through the night with no change in intensity.

At about 5am my little girl pottered into our room as she normally did, walked around to my side of the bed and kissed me on the nose before indicating she wanted to come in between my partner and I. She then proceeded to tell me all about her previous day in her three year old way. She had missed the opportunity the evening before and needed to make amends. Her language and enthusiasm always made me laugh. As I giggled my pain went. She had pushed my happy app and everything changed.

As a physical therapist this was one of the most profound and informing experiences I have had. I was fortunate enough to know which part of my body was in spasm, and how to position myself to relieve it. This was my first ex-

Live a Life That is Limitless

perience of back pain. I had never had a twinge my whole life. The experience had given me an insight into how the many patients I have treated over the years were actually feeling, and more importantly, a conformation of how consciousness affects our bodies. We can't help having our Reactor Apps tapped, but we do have a choice whether we continue running the app or choose something different.

In this experience my facilitator for change was my daughter. She changed my state from anger to one of happiness. She snapped the anger junky cycle I was running. The continuous stream of justification I was using to keep taking the Anger peptide hit all through the night. Using the Blame App to tap the Anger App clearly wasn't going to be enough this time. I needed pain to add to the trauma and drama which helped to reinforce the distraction. Nothing like a bit of pain to distract you from just about everything.

Anger, Frustration and Blame hits from my "Interesting Thoughts"
"Can't believe she did that to me!"

"She didn't even say thank you!"
"Can't believe she made me waste an hour for no reason!"
"Can't believe she used our company time and staff to organise someone else's event!"
"And didn't even get paid for it!"
"Then she expects me to pick up the kids AND make dinner!"
"Fuck this hurts!!"
"Now I have to stop what I'm doing and waste more time stretching!"
"Don't you DARE even talk to me!!"
"I'm going to bed .. DON'T! touch me!"
"NO! I don't want drugs leave me alone!"
"Fuck this hurts see what you've done!"

Happiness, Love and Gratitude hits from my daughter.
"Morning Dada". (kiss on the nose)
"Chloe have cuddle please"
"Mmmm snuggly bear … I love you"
"Chloe drew a picture yesterday dada"
"You want to see it?" " It's pretty…"

CHAPTER TEN

Understanding Our Conditioning

The Foundations

Our conditioning starts from the moment we are conceived. Every emotion our mother experiences while we are in her womb begins to mould the foundations of how we cope in the world once we are born. The mother's emotional experiences are imprinted in the baby. The more stressful the environment for the mother during the pregnancy, the more likely the child's brain development will default to favour the limbic system. This child will be born with a strong grip and ability to hold on tight to the mother in any situation and tends to only be interested in learning what it will need to survive. The Calmer the pregnancy and birth the more likely the child's brain

development pathways will
favour a more cortical development of the brain. This child can be physically weaker and usually develops a fascination and love for learning and enjoys school.

Once we are born we are in download mode for the first 9 years. Everything we see and hear is downloaded. There is no conceptualisation, no rationalisation. Just download and copy. Some call it the hypnogogic phase. So everything your child sees and hears before the Rubicon phase (8-9 years of age) is downloaded and stored ready to be accessed again once conceptualisation begins.

This is where most of the mimicry starts. We mimic the influential people around us: Our parents and siblings, teachers and friends. We also mimic characters in books, films and TV. We then spend the rest of our lives measuring how well we are mimicking. The measurement we use is Judgement. We judge ourselves in ways we are probably not even aware of. When we don't feel we measure up to the crap we have in our data base we become insecure. We feel not good enough or a failure. We then

Live a Life That is Limitless

think everyone else is judging us in the same way, and so the cycle of the limitation of Judgement, Trauma and Drama continues.

How We Are Conditioned Through Education

The education systems around the world have evolved over the last couple of hundred years into very effective systems for conditioning our children and societies through a set way of learning. Education has become mainstream with slight variations in compulsory attendance age ranges. Currently the UK has the widest range where children commence age five and finish age 17. This law will be changed again in 2015 when children will stay until they are 18. Most other first world countries have similar age ranges for compulsory education.

The way we are educated teaches us to read, write and understand numbers. This is fine, after all mathematics is pure, I guess it falls in the category of Universal Law. Languages have their specific rules which need to be learnt so we are able to read and write. It's not so much the subjects that condition us, it's the subconscious conditioning that is created from the way the system is delivered. During formative years in standard education we are taught in a linear way. Every year we are taught the same things the previous years were taught. Subject matter may change on rare occasions but the delivery stays the same. It works most of the time. Most children learn enough of the information to execute the most important part of their conditioning.

To answer questions on the subjects, in the order the information has been taught.

Questions are usually formulated by the teacher from the text books which have been used during the term. Questions are usually given in the order they where taught. This is the linear learning process which is the opposite to how our brain actually functions.

So we go to school, are taught interesting and sometimes non interesting subjects, and then are expected to answer questions on those subjects in the order they where taught. When we answer the questions correctly we pass

Live a Life That is Limitless

and are able to move onto the next level to do the same thing over again with more information. As we mature into tertiary education we are given even more books accompanied by the odd lecture, and told to study the books and anything else we can get our hands on relevant to that subject. Then we are given more questions and asked to answer the questions and discuss the reasons we have come up with, to justify our answers. Eventually if we stay in education long enough we are able to choose our own questions to answer, providing the person marking the question knows enough about it so they can make sure we are not wrong.

How cool is that?

You start by having to answer the same questions everyone else does and finish by choosing a question you would like to find the answer too. When you get this far you get to have letters before and after your name and everyone wants to ask you even more questions. You can choose to spend your time answering heaps of questions, teach others all about the answers you have discovered, or totally ignore them because they aren't clever enough to ask you in the first place, and probably wouldn't understand your answer anyway. By the time you reach school leaving age, you have been conditioned in two main ways.

1. To do as you are told:

You are told what to learn and by when. You are told when to eat and what is and is not acceptable. You are told what you can and cannot wear, what language is not acceptable and in many cases what to believe and what not to believe. You are given strict rules to follow, which conditions you to do as you are told, whether you like it or not.

2. To give the right answer:

"What is the right answer? If you don't give the right answer you will fail".

Fear of failure undermines self worth and pushes most individuals into a reptilian mode of learning. This is when you become only interested in learning what you need to pass the test.

Live a Life That is Limitless

"Tell me what I need to know to pass the exam".
"Tell me what I need to know to give the right answers and I'll do it".

Any flicker of excitement towards education that may have existed is extinguished. We can only choose from a hand full of subjects, many of which may not interest us at all. This sets us up by limiting our choices. We can only take the courses that are offered, which pushes most people into learning things they are not really interested in. They end up in jobs and careers they find most unfulfilling.

The joy of learning new and exciting things is undermined and you find getting the right answer a bore and a grind or extremely stressful. You start to look for answers and if you can't find the right answer you ask someone who you deem to be as clever or cleverer than you. This conditioning creates a state where you are continuously looking for the right answer in everything you do. Justification through the limitations of the knowledge you have.

The fundamental limitation with all of this is your 'Body Console' only knows what it knows, so it can only ever discover answers and make decisions from the limitations of its current knowledge base. You can only research and formulate questions from the limitations of the education you have or the education you have access too. A knowledge base most of which the vast majority of people are probably not really interested in.

This sounds obvious but take a moment to think back to the first conversation you read in this book. When I asked Anna if she had a soul she said yes and acknowledged that it was infinite. She recognised a part of herself as an 'Infinite Being' and understood that an 'Infinite Being' would already know everything.

The conversation concluded with me saying "YOU' knows EVERYTHING ...... Anna Console is just not AWARE of EVERYTHING. Her brain doesn't have the capacity to hold all of that information at once. However, she can access any part of the EVERYTHING by simply asking questions."

Live a Life That is Limitless

Our conditioning has been to find the right answers. We are taught to use rationale and logic to measure all probabilities. Find what is most likely to be the 'Right' answer to make it legitimate. Historically, once enough people agreed, one could claim superiority over anyone else who didn't understand.

Answering our own questions works in a limited way. How much more could we create and be, if we were to ask questions without falling into the conditioning of having to find the right answer?

Albert Einstein once said:
"The intuitive mind is a sacred gift and the rational mind is a faithful servant. We have created a society that honours the servant and has forgotten the gift"

The infinite part of ourselves already knows everything there is to know. It is as if we have been born with a membership card to the library of infinite knowledge. Our membership card is our (Right Brain) intuitive mind. When we ask questions without trying to find the right answer, we swipe our way in to the library and access infinite possibilities we could never have imagined.

This is 'The Gift'. Conditioning yourself into a new constant awareness of how to use 'The Gift' is the moment you start to create a life that's fun and easy.

CHAPTER ELEVEN

Ten Study Steps to Break The Limitations of Linear Learning.

The education system is linear learning. This is where the brain is trained to take in information in a specific order. We are given information in a logical sequence which is supposed to be the best way to learn. The problem is, our brains don't function in this way naturally. Our brains are highly dense bundles of multi directional neurones with no linear pathways. This is why some people struggle so much with mainstream education. A Universi-

Live a Life That is Limitless

ty in Canada split one year group in two for their final year examination. Group 1's paper had questions compiled in the order they had been taught. Group 2's examination paper was compiled using a randomised question order. All questions on both papers where the same. Group 2 students took three times longer to complete their exams, where their questions had not been presented in the order they were taught.

Awareness is everything. Once you are aware how the education system is set up to condition you, you can change how you view the system. Knowledge conquers fear. Knowledge is power. Are statements that have been used for centuries. Better to say Awareness conquers fear, and Awareness is power. Once you are aware of how to play the system you can never fail and you can use the system to your advantage.

Breaking the linear learning conditioning is easier than you might think. The secret is to develop multiple pathways in your brain, to a single piece of information. If you are currently at school or in university, do the following for every subject you are taking and you will never fail. Hint … the people who use this method get A's for everything, every time, no matter how much time they have to study.

"Do the following" means do it exactly as I state here.

1. For each subject: Compile your subject notes into the exact order they were taught to you.

2. Work out how much study time you will need for each subject before your exam (e.g. 1hr per subject per study period).

3. Split the period of time you have from now until the day of your exam into four phases. (e.g. 4 x 2.5 weeks).

4. Split each of your subject notes into ten equal piles keeping them in the exact order they were taught to you. If you are at the beginning of a semester create the ten piles as you go. Work out the content for each

Live a Life That is Limitless

pile from your semester time table.

5. Phase 1: During your allotted study period, start with your first pile and read each pile 1-10 of your notes through once only in the order they were taught to you.

6. Phase 2: During your allotted study period, start with your tenth pile and read each pile of notes 10 - 1 through once only in the reverse order they were taught to you.

7. Phase 3: Each time you study during phase 3 mix up the ten equal piles of notes into a different random order. (e.g. 731496258) During your allotted study period, read each pile of notes through once only in the new random order you chose before you start each study period.

8. Phase 4: For each study period. Split all the ten piles of notes down into single sheets and mix them all together. Every study period, create ten totally new random piles of notes. Read each pile of notes

through once only in the random order you created before you started studying.

9. Only use the time you have planned for each subject.. Don't let your mind wonder off. Keep your concentration read for twenty minutes break for five.

10. For languages, maths, physics and chemistry subjects, learn the rules of the game first. Then practice applying them. The people who fail these subjects have not learned the rules properly.

By following the process above for information that has been delivered in a linear way, you start to establish multiple pathways in the brain for all aspects of the information taught to you, rather than a single pathway through the order in which you have been taught. This makes it much easier to recall everything you need to during your exams.

Question Everything the Education System Has to Offer and always Follow The Money.

Live a Life That is Limitless

Who wrote the syllabus?
Who prints the books and who owns the printer?
Who publishes the books and who owns the publishing house?
Who contributes to the university and how much?
What research ideas have been turned down and why?
Who is funding the current research programmes and why?

Always ask for the other side of the story.
This is his-story, what does the other side say?
What natural product does this medicine originate from and why aren't we using it?
What research results have not been published because the law says they Don't have to be?
Who owns the patent?
Who funded the patent?
How much does it cost to manufacture?
How much is it sold for?
Who do the profits go to?
Who gave the owners the money?
Where is astro turfing being used?
Where is there no regulation and why?

Who does the non regulation benefit most?

Attend your linear learning programme so you can give in the right answers. Build your awareness by asking questions like the ones posed above for everything you are ever taught through the education system. Keep asking questions and follow the money. You will be surprised what you find.

CHAPTER TWELVE

Asking without trying to find the right answer.

Asking questions without trying to find the right answer, is the most effective way to create the level of awareness that will enable us to actualise the changes we wish to experience in life. What, Can and How are the three main questions one can use to start creating awareness and change. Be careful how you construct your questions. Use

Live a Life That is Limitless

words not intension. What we say we create. Intension is nothing but an idea we haven't actioned, it is always in the future. Asking questions is in the now and uses a different awareness.

A couple of years ago my relationship with my partner was struggling. There was a lot of anger and resentment between us because of past events (nothing to do with the previous story…). At the time I was writing a book, practicing part time, learning astrology, studying a Doctorate in Alternative Medicine and looking after my kids while my partner advanced her career. While using my Personal Focus System I ask the following question without trying to find the right answer.

"What would my <u>relationship</u> look like if there was no anger?"

The key word in this question was 'Relationship'. My intension was to seek an answer about how my relationship with my partner would look like if there was no anger. I didn't specify that verbally, so suffered the consequences which actually created far more clarity for me than I initially intended.

It took me four weeks to finally realise my question had been answered some four weeks previously. Looking back I realised, soon after I asked the question I experienced a sudden drop in my motivation to do any of the things I was doing. Education, private practice and writing all stopped. I remember sitting in my astrology class asking what the point of learning astrology was. I had no motivation at all. I realised my question had been answered exactly as I had asked. I had been shown what my 'relationship' with everything would look like with no anger.

Traditional Chinese Medicine gives the best analogy of the importance of anger. This ancient system says Anger is generated by the Liver and Gallbladder (Wood Element). Anger is the motivational energy we have pulsing through our bodies. Anger energy is what gets us out of bed in the morning, keeps us motivated and drives us forward every day and most of all anger protects us from feeling fear. This is not necessarily the peptide that is produced by the anger App. The anger App is only ever

Live a Life That is Limitless

tapped when there is a lie present or a Truth with a lie attached. I was shown what my relationship with my children, study, patients, car, shoes, food, books, everything would be like with no anger. The loss of motivation created a depressive state. The question had been so generic I had become distracted with all the other demonstrations of how things in my world would be with no anger.

I should have asked:

"What would my relationship with (partners name) be like if there was no anger?"

The original question created the awareness of what is a Truth for me, by taking all the motivation away from everything I was doing. This created awareness of how everything actually was for me rather than how I thought it was.

The justifications I had made to prioritise doing a doctorate and write a book were shown for what they were. The whole process created an immense amount of clarity for me once I realised the depressive state was just me being shown what everything looks like without the motivation of the belief systems and IT's I had bought into. Until then I had been putting my main focus on the Doctorate. I realised I was having far more fun writing books, writing Personal Focus System and Performance Enhancement Visualisation workshops and treating people, than I was doing the Doctorate. So I swopped things round and made writing the priority, and the doctorate something I can do for fun at a later date.

Access Consciousness with Gary Douglas has contributed hugely to my awareness of the importance of asking questions. Some of the questions that are asked in this system are as follows.
- What choices do I need to be aware of that will create the changes I'm seeking…..?
- Can I create more of this in my life?
- How can I create more of this in my life?
- What do I need to perceive, know, be and receive now?
- What Question, Choice, Possibility and Contribution can I be now?
- What else is possible?
- Who else is possible?

Live a Life That is Limitless
- How does it get any better than this?

Once your question has been answered, if you are happy with your answer ask:

How does it get any better than this and what else is possible?

If you are unhappy with you answer, ask:

How does it get any better than this and what else is possible?

CHAPTER THIRTEEN

What We Say We Create

People use positive affirmations to help facilitate change in their world. So do they work? Yes if you are aware of exactly what you are saying and don't include intension. When we remain aware of exactly what we say, we create the vibration or frequency of energy Einstein was talking about. If we are not totally aligned to that energy we will not actualise what we are saying. Being totally aligned to the energetic vibration we are creating with words becomes most powerful when we are not attached to any outcome.

Live a Life That is Limitless

Most affirmations are something someone else has said. What works for them isn't necessarily going to work for you. Saying what you are choosing now, is a more consistent way of creating momentum and positive change in your world. When you say what you are choosing and have no point of view about the outcome.

This means when we make the positive statement like; Today I am choosing to feel good about myself. Make the statement without any preconceived ideas about what is going to happen that will make you happy. Just make the statement and see what shows up in your world.

Now I am choosing to feel good about myself.
Today I am choosing to be happy.
Now I am choosing to receive my truth with ease.
Today I am choosing to have fun.

Once you verbally state your choice, you begin to actualise that choice by projecting your vibration through what you have just said. If you have said 'Now I am choosing to be happy', the vibration you have projected will actualise situations that make you happy through your day.

The I AM's are powerful too.
I AM money.
I AM abundance in all things that are a truth for me.
I AM happy.
I AM perfect health.
I AM total allowance.

Understanding the language we use every day is critical in helping us stay focused and moving forward creating little or no obstacles. When we use a word like "Goal" we are usually describing what we would like to achieve. So there is an unvoiced intension within the description we verbalise. The unvoiced intension has not actually been Said. This can create an energetic contradiction. The longest recorded meaning for the word Goal is "obstacle, barrier," or "to hinder." (Goal Longest recorded meaning from 14th Century Old English *gal "obstacle, barrier," a word implied by gælan "to hinder." http://www.etymonline.com).

Live a Life That is Limitless

It is the longest meaning of a word that holds the strongest meaning in consciousness. Goal has been in the English language probably longer than we have written records for. If there is doubt in your intension it may not be strong enough to over ride the original meaning. Your Goal then becomes an obstacle or barrier to your success. One which you will have to conquer before you can move on. Obstacles, barriers and hindrances stick us and distract us. How many times in our lives have we created unnecessary barriers for ourselves through the 'Goals' we have set.

Some regularly used words and their meanings.

Limiting word: Goal Longest recorded meaning from 14th Century Old English *gal "obstacle, barrier," a word implied by gælan "to hinder."

Alternate word: Target
Longest recorded meaning; English, French, Frankish and Nordic - a light shield. German - edging or boundary.

Limiting word: Intend. (I intend to - is in the future) .... c. 1300, "direct one's attention to," from Old French entendre, intendre "to direct one's attention" (in Modern French principally "to hear"), from Latin intendere "turn one's attention, strain," literally "stretch out, extend," from in- "toward"

Alternate word: Choose. (I am choosing to - is in the now).
12th Century. Old English ceosan "choose, seek out, select; decide, test, taste, try; accept, approve" (class II strong verb; past tense ceas, past participle coren), from Proto-Germanic *keus- (cf. Old Frisian kiasa, Old Saxon kiosan, Dutch kiezen, Old High German kiosan, German kiesen, Old Norse kjosa, Gothic kiusan "choose," Gothic kausjan "to taste, test"),
Choice was described as the "Power of Choosing" since the 1300's.

Limiting word: Passion: late 12c., "sufferings of Christ on the Cross," from Old French passion "Christ's passion, physical suffering" (10c.), from Late Latin passionem (nominative passio) "suffering, enduring," from past participle stem of Latin pati "to suffer, endure," possibly from PIE root *pe(i)- "to hurt" (cf. Sanskrit pijati "reviles, scorns," Greek pema "suffering, misery, woe," Old English

Live a Life That is Limitless

feond "enemy, devil," Gothic faian "to blame"). Passionate: early 15c., "angry; emotional," from Medieval Latin passionatus "affected with passion," from Latin passio (genitive passionis) "passion" (see passion). Specific sense of "amorous" is attested from 1580s. Related: Passionately.

So what happened to Christ? He was betrayed, arrested, scorned, interrogated, judged, tortured, humiliated, suffered and crucified. Which of these aspects of 'Passion' has shown up while you were doing what you say you are most passionate about?

Alternative choice: I love to.
(www.etymonline.com)

CHAPTER FOURTEEN

"Where do you see yourself in five years?"

This is a common question asked. Of course we then go off in our conditioned minds using the limited knowledge base we have, to come up with ideas we think are right for us. Mostly ego driven concepts of where we would like to live, how much money we would like to have, a first class seat around the world, flashy car, enough money to never have to worry about money again, perfect partner who loves sex and is good at it, a fit body with plenty of spare time to have fun, and so on.

Once you have identified what you would like to achieve in five years (as if achieving it all now would be totally impossible) you are usually encouraged to set 'Goals'. During this phase it is generally those who have no idea of how they will achieve their vision that are

Live a Life That is Limitless

the most successful. These individuals are also the ones who piss everyone else off because they seem to have outrageous ideas far beyond their station and nothing to back them up.

If creating a vision board, you usually find photos and pictures on the net or in glossy magazines that seem to fit the 'Goals' you have determined you will need to reach at various stages over the coming five years. We slot into the logical world of what would be possible in the given time frame of five years. As we do this we inadvertently start to impose limitations on ourselves from the beginning. This is not a bad thing or even the wrong way to go about achieving your so called 'Goals'. In fact vision boards do actually work quite well, and are fun to put together.

The limitations we inadvertently impose on ourselves are like the small print in a legal document. Everyone is aware the small print exists but not many people take the time to sit down and read everything until they understand it. Then when something goes wrong, they end up having to pay far more than they would have if they had chosen to be informed in the first place. In the case of the vision board it is the fine print we impose on ourselves that chokes the possibilities we are trying to create. We end up paying far more in time as it takes longer to actualise the things we are wishing for.

Most self development programmes and courses focus on goal setting and what you would like to achieve in your life. Some use vision boards while others teach visualisation techniques, not too different from the system I will be teaching you in part two. For me, the fundamental difference between us and them is how we recognise the limitations that are created through our conditioning. When we can focus from a place where we hold no point of view about an outcome we can start to negate any hidden fine print from our conditioning. This is where we start to choose from awareness not reaction.

As I mentioned before, flicking the 'A' switch is where our power is. You cannot fix something if you are not aware it is broken. Likewise you cannot actualise something if you

Live a Life That is Limitless

are not aware of your potential to do so. Once we become aware the small print exists and what it actually is, we can change the way we do things by not creating the small print in the same way.

In the vision board example above the small print is hidden in the process in a number of subtle but powerfully limiting ways.

lets take a quick look at the question:

Where do you see yourself in five years?

Here are two of the ways we automatically start limiting ourselves when this question is asked.

1. Because of our conditioning, asking this question locks you straight into the 'Rational Mind'. Your conditioning forces you to find the right answer under your current circumstances using your current knowledge base. So you create an answer that seems feasible under your current circumstances.

2. Five years is a finite amount of time. Focussing on a finite amount of time locks us into the 'Rational Mind' where our logic tells us only certain things would be possible to achieve within that time frame, because we are "only human after all". If we don't achieve our goals within the allotted time we are a failure. Then we can blame the process and say it doesn't work.

CHAPTER FIFTEEN

Choice and Your Universal Stamp.

Everything that happens to us in life is due to the choices we have made at any given moment. Unfortunately our conditioning plays an integral role in influencing us in what and how we choose.

Live a Life That is Limitless

When we have been conditioned to do as we are told, this creates the belief we don't have a choice.

When we are conditioned to give the right answer this creates a belief we don't have any other choice but the Right one.

Would an infinite being not have a choice?

Would an infinite being not know an answer that would create total ease?

So what are you choosing today that will create a life of total ease for you now and in the future?

What can I choose now that will create $10,000.00 by the end of this month?

What choice can I be here that will connect me with this person?

Choice is all we have. Some say there is no choice at all because the planets say so. Consciousness is ever evolving and when you are born it's as if your body is Stamped by the universe. That Stamp is a depiction of where everything is in our solar system at the moment of our birth. This will dictate how everything will unfold in our lives and we have no control over how any of it will turn out.

I agree.. We are 'Stamped' by the universe the moment we are born. This 'Stamp' will always give us our characteristics, personality types and fundamental nature. What our bodies are vulnerable too and when we are likely to become ill and heal. When we will marry and whether someone has a predisposition to being unfaithful. Whether we will be active and good at sport or more reflective, academic and thoughtful. These aspects and many more can be calculated mathematically with extreme accuracy. These are the characteristics of your Game Console. Like a gamer choosing how your character will dress, what colour skin and hair your character will have and what the gender will be. As each game console has been created with the same Reactor Apps, the 'Stamp" defines how likely you are to use certain Reactor

Live a Life That is Limitless

Apps, and how and where your game console will play in the mainframe.

I believe our body console still has freedom of choice once it has become aware of the Stamp and how our conditioning contributes to our story. If we stay in Reaction, we fall victim to the aspects of the "Stamp" unique to our story which are enhanced and perpetuated through the ways we have been conditioned. Constant distraction through a combination of the "Stamp" and our conditioning.

We remain distracted from real choice because we are too busy reacting to the story we are playing at the time. Once we flick the 'A' Switch and are no longer distracted, we create enough space in our world to recognise when and how the Stamp and our conditioning is working, and how to counter or absorb the effects. We also get to a place where we can no longer be influenced or controlled by our conditioning.

The Tunnel Analogy

I like to use another analogy for our journey through life. It is like being born at the back of a huge tunnel. The tunnel is our life path or "Stamp". A theatre that is totally unique to our body console and the challenges our 'YOU' is here to face. Although the exit is in one direction, there are many ways to it. We can choose any route we like. Each choice will always be influenced by the tunnel we are in.

We will be more likely to choose difficult routes while we are in a traumatic Reaction. Those routes will usually provide the biggest challenges on our journey. Going back over the same path is pointless, every time we do this we trip up and slow ourselves down. This is when we are being the Peptaholic, when our addiction to the peptide is running our Body Console. This is when we believe we don't have a choice. The more we are in Reaction and believe we don't have a choice, the more likely we will be to take the roughest path.

The less Reaction we are in, the more likely we will see every path for what it is, and choose the route that is

Live a Life That is Limitless

most fun and light for us. In the end, we will always reach the light at the end of the tunnel, even if we have not learned everything we could have along the way. Most importantly our 'YOU' has never been wrong or right, good or bad.

So Choose what is light and follow your Truth, it is the easiest path to ease and abundance in everything you experience traveling through your tunnel.

Anna: What is my Truth?

John: Choosing to do what you truly love to do, not what someone else thinks would be good for you.

CHAPTER SIXTEEN

Overcoming Judgement

A colleague of mine used to enjoy telling of an experience she had while living in a large city in South America. One evening she was out for dinner with friends in a very affluent part of town. The restaurant was packed with exceptionally wealthy people enjoying the atmosphere and food. On this particular evening an armed gang entered the restaurant, and began to relieve everyone of their wallets, jewellery and anything else they decided was worth taking. Shocked, everyone gave up their valuables. Before leaving, the gang stopped at the door, aimed their automatic weapons at the guests and said "Everybody strip naked, anyone who doesn't will be shot."

Live a Life That is Limitless

Of course everyone stripped naked, and stood in all their glory as the gang disappeared. I don't recall if she mentioned if they were ever caught or not, but the story did make me smile. As the exceptionally wealthy stood naked in the restaurant after being robbed, they no longer wore the masks that defined them within their society. The movie stars, executives, bankers, politicians, doctors and lawyers. At that moment their position in society did not matter. They could no longer hide behind designer clothing. The personal items that enhanced the way they looked and displayed their wealth would soon be divided up by the thieves and reimbursed by the insurance companies. For the few minutes they stood unmasked they were no different to the men who robbed them, the beggar on the street or any other human being in the world.

Not many of us are truly ever naked. We have been brought up for the most part to believe it is wrong to be seen naked. In most societies public nudity is illegal and in some, even uncovering your face will get you publicly executed. As infants and toddlers we run naked and free with no inhibitions about our bodies and who we are. As we grow and become more aware of who we are we become more self conscious. We are then told to cover ourselves up because being naked is wrong and people will laugh at us. The natural blooming of a healthy body starts to be hidden and become embarrassing. We begin to judge ourselves by comparing how we look to those around us.

Society has been conditioned through guilt and fear. Religion deems the body to be a sacred vessel, yet if you enjoy the ultimate physical vibration of an orgasm too much you are a sinner. Succumb to the pleasures of the flesh and you will be damned for all eternity. Society then creates laws that support the religion based guilt and fear mongering about the wrongness of our bodies.

So we remain covered unless behind closed doors. In many cases we change out of the clothing we are wearing and don the protection and security of the room we are in. The wrongness that has become our bodies remains hidden from the world, and we feel safe from ridicule. The more layers we wear the less likely we will receive ridicule and judgement of our bodies. The less clothing we wear the more vulnerable we become.

Live a Life That is Limitless

Have you ever noticed something about yourself that you really didn't want anyone else to notice, but every time you interacted with people they pointed it out?

When we wake up in the morning and look in the mirror and judge our body consoles to be 'not good enough', we start setting ourselves up to be judged. Once we align ourselves to the judgments we make about our bodies, we create an energetic projection around us that other people can hook into. Because we have judged ourselves to be wrong in some way, we then walk out into the world assuming everyone else is judging us in the same way.

People can only judge us from the judgements we project about ourselves. It is the projections we have created that everyone else hooks into. Our energetic projection of self judgement seems to attract those people who will notice the same things about us we have made wrong about ourselves. Conveniently pointing out to us and everyone else our problem. When we no longer judge ourselves we can't be judged, people have nothing to hook into so don't bother trying.

CHAPTER SEVENTEEN

Creating Vulnerability

People shy away from vulnerability. Understanding vulnerability and how it can empower you is extremely liberating, and creates a place of inner confidence. Embracing vulnerability will always lead to a place of no judgement. When I say vulnerability, I don't mean taking yourself off to some war torn area of the world to start walking through sniper infested streets hoping you don't get shot that is just insane.

Vulnerable in this context is the vulnerability you feel when you have judged yourself to be not good enough and are afraid for the judgement to be seen by others. We all

Live a Life That is Limitless

have things we have done that we wish we had not. Most of the time, very few people know about this one thing we are ashamed of. Some people may have multiple things they have done they are ashamed of. What would happen if you were summoned to a court to justify yourself in front of your friends, peers and family. How does that thought make you feel? To be put on a witness stand and be interrogated in front of everyone you know. Let's find out.

CHAPTER EIGHTEEN

The Court Room.

Think of an occasion when you chose to do something you really wish you had not. Maybe it was a one off, or something you did regularly over a specific period of time. The key here is to choose an experience you have had which you would not like anyone else to know about. Something that makes you embarrassed to even think about. Something that makes you cringe. How would you feel if the people closest too you found out about it? What would you have to say to justify your actions? Do you even know why you chose to do or behave in that specific way at that time?

Fill the court room with everyone you know. Friends, family members, and people you respect and who respect you. How about including your church congregation (they will

Live a Life That is Limitless

judge the fuck out of you!!), school teachers, lecturers, grandparents. If you teach, how about including your students and their parents.

Have the person you despise the most in your life as the prosecution and the weakest most timid person you know as your defence. Put a Judge in place if you like.

Step into the box and allow yourself to be questioned. What would be the worst most embarrassing questions anyone could ask you regarding your story? Allow those questions to be asked by the person you despise the most. What pleasure would they take in humiliating you?

Which Reactor Apps are being pushed?

There will be combinations which create unique peptide recipes you can experience. Flavour combinations of Anger. Hate, Blame, Fury, Shame,
Guilt, Regret, Sex, Relationships, Money, Business, Perversions, Addictions and Compulsions.
Remember it is just a peptide that makes you feel the experience. How do they make you feel?

How would you answer each question that comes up?
How would you justify your actions?
You chose what you chose for what reason?

Don't apologise, Just mention that everyone makes choices they have regretted and this is one of those times. Continue answering the questions until you no longer feel any reactor apps running. No regret, no embarrassment. This may take a few minutes or you may cry everyday for a week. Either way you are releasing the emotional charge created by the belief systems you have used to play that story out. The insane beliefs you used to choose that insanity in the first place. As you play this out in your mind, begin to allow yourself to be judged. Stand in the box and smile to everyone in the court room. Smile at your prosecutor, the person you despise the most in your life, standing in front of you taking this fantastic opportunity to humiliate you totally. Smile at your family, colleagues, students, parents and everyone else present.
Then say to everyone: JTFOOM... (Jit Foom).

Live a Life That is Limitless

CHAPTER NINETEEN

"JTFOOM!"

Anna: How is your mirror working?
John: Fuckin 'A'!

Once you have started connecting with your body console you will find you begin to judge yourself less and less every day. Once we no longer judge our Body Consoles to be faulty we create the space and the ability to be vulnerable enough to allow ourselves to be judged by anyone. Once you allow yourself to be judged, you can not be, and the distraction created from the emotional reactions you locked yourself into will disappear.

Using a mirror is an effective way to start connecting with your body. There are many quotes and statements made about loving the self. The message is usually the same. When you love yourself, only then can you experience true love. By loving ourselves unconditionally we create a space where we can receive with ease. Being able to receive with ease perpetuates the cycle of joy that is created when we give and receive. Loving and honouring ourselves shuts down self judgement. It's the self judgement that we project into our world that people hook into to judge us. When you love yourself and no longer judge yourself no-one has anything to hook into and you cannot be judged. JTFOOM is an effective tool you can have a lot of fun with once you start using it.

Lets continue with the analogy of the YOU and the Body Console and constantly referred to our bodies in the first person. In the following chapters I will explain muscle testing and how you can develop that sense for yourself. Let's start by first taking more notice of our bodies and start acknowledge how utterly amazing they are.

Stand naked in front of the biggest mirror you can find. Start by standing relaxed and look into your own eyes. Hold your gaze and don't look anywhere else until you can

Live a Life That is Limitless

hold your own gaze for 5 minutes. Once you have connected with yourself, step back and start to admire your body. Say thank you to your body console for loving and supporting YOU from the moment of birth to the moment the body chooses to die. Think of all the significant things you have both achieved. How amazing is this body console. Ask "how you doing today?" "What would you like to achieve today? " Say thanks for all the sporting, academic, creative achievements you have been given the opportunity to experience. Has she given birth? How amazing is that!! How she feels when she swims, runs, climbs. Have fun with him in the mirror. Turn and look at her back, front, and sides. Tell her she has perfect hair, eyes, nose, lips, shoulders, breasts, nipples, and tummy. Keep going until you have mentioned all the parts of your body out loud and with a smile. The body only looks the way it does because it keeps itself alive for YOU. Every decision YOU makes has to be processed by the body so the body can stay alive as long as possible.

YOU gets to play the game with this awesome body console until the body has had enough. So tell her you love her and how proud you are of her for achieving so many amazing things. Look deep into his eyes with pride and tell him how awesome he is.

Once you have done this a few times you will begin to feel what it is like to not judge yourself. This is when JTFOOM will begin to work for you.

Judge The Fuck Out Of Me!! (JTFOOM)

Once you have started connecting with your body console you will find you begin to judge yourself less and less every day. Once we no longer judge our Body Consoles to be faulty we create the space and the ability to be vulnerable enough to allow ourselves to be totally judged by anyone. Once you allow yourself to be totally judged … you can't be…. and the distraction created from the emotional reactions you have been locked into will disappear.

Take JTFOOM out into your world every day. Say JTFOOM when you walk into a cafe or restaurant, board room or business meeting. Every time you go out on a date or interact with total strangers. Every time you get eye con-

Live a Life That is Limitless

tact with someone you have never met think JTFOOM. Visualise yourself naked in the process and JTFOOM. Imagine how their face would look if you were actually naked. How do you think they would react to your vulnerability and continue saying JTFOOM. You will begin to notice there is no reaction to you. You cannot be judged. You will notice this creates a subtle conflict for them. When they first caught sight of you they will have automatically tried to form an opinion about you by hooking into the projections of self judgement you usually have. While you are JTFOOMing, those projections no longer exist so their confusion is subconscious and they are not quite sure what is going on. There is something different about you but they can't quite put their finger on it. When this happens you will notice it straight away. That's the moment you known you have nailed JTFOOM.

CHAPTER TWENTY

Choosing from Innate

The innate wisdom of the body is the different levels of the subconscious mind. Albert Einstein described the subconscious mind as "The Gift". That part of the mind where there are no limitations. I have found the results people create for themselves when tapping into the subconscious mind to be amazing, a humbling experience for both practitioner and patient alike. It is a paradigm in thinking and approach to not only healthcare but life in general. Connecting and communicating with the Innate of an individual can be established quite simply through muscle testing.

Bio Feed Back or Muscle Testing
Muscle testing is another phenomenon which has been comprehensively researched within alternative medicine.

Live a Life That is Limitless

Chiropractors and Applied Kinesiology practitioners have used it since 1967. The Bodytalk System which is the main modality I use has been established for 20 years and is in over 35 countries to date. The muscle test is the most effective way of by passing the limitations of the conscious mind. By setting the body up to respond a specific way for Yes and the opposite for No we can then tap into the innate knowledge of our bodies for information we could not have otherwise considered. This is our direct link to our sub conscious mind and can be done anytime in both Beta or Alpha states. This only works with closed questioning. i.e. Questions that must be answered with Yes or No.

Ask:
Body Show me YES
Body Show me NO

I personally prefer to set my body up to sway forward for YES and backwards for NO. Once you
have practiced this a number of times you will feel the forward/backward sensation very clearly. This will help

you create clarity when you are unsure whether a choice is light or heavy.

Sensing:
Light is a Truth, Heavy is a Lie.

Choosing from a place you sense is Light will always create results faster than you could ever expect. When you sense a choice to be light, it will make you smile and your body will buzz and respond with ease. As I said in earlier in this book, truth is a Universal Law and cannot be hidden. A question preceded by the word 'truth' will elicit an honest response. I gave the example of the young child whose answer will usually be "Yes NO!" when you pose them a question like "Truth, did you paint this picture on the wall?" Adults and older children will pause for a second before they go ahead to tell the truth. Your body is no different. She will sway forward for yes, or create the sensation of being pulled forward or drawn to something. This sensation will start to increase in intensity the more you practice. Soon you will feel the pull towards people, situations and objects your body will enjoy interacting with.

Live a Life That is Limitless

When you choose something that you sense is Heavy it is usually a lie for you. When we choose Heavy, results happen far slower, usually with barriers, the enjoyment tends to be lost and every
thing turns into a grind. We have a tendency to over rationalise which sticks us and chokes the flow through over analysis. This is when your body will be showing you NO. You can feel physically pulled away from the person or situation. Like a friend is pulling you backwards by your shirt, or for the most part the sensation may be subtly drawing you away. This should not be underestimated or ignored. One of my colleagues taught this to a patient with a serious heart condition. After his latest check up with his physician he was prescribed some new heart medication. He decided to ask his body if he would like to take the meds. The first time he asked he was holding the meds against his chest. His body flew backwards quite violently. He kept asking and kept getting a very strong no. He phoned my colleague up and asked her advice on the matter. She insisted he get a second opinion for another physician. On doing so he found he had been pre-

scribed the wrong medication and he was told if he had taking the pills they would have killed him.

Keep practicing this and you will blow yourself away with the results you start to create. This approach to making choices is favouring the most powerful aspect of self which is the subconscious mind. You bypass the left brain which holds your belief systems. The limitations you impose on yourself. By practicing this everyday it will soon become second nature, and your intuition will sharpen.

CHAPTER TWENTY ONE

Summary of Part 1

1. 'YOU' is the infinite being in all of us that knows everything. Your Body Console is a finite being and does not have the capacity to know everything.

2. Every belief has been created by judging an interesting thought (IT) to be right, good, wrong or bad. We are limiting ourselves when we judge something to be right, good, wrong or bad.

3. Every Belief has Reactor Apps attached to it.

4. Each Reactor App has a series of peptide recipes attached to them.

5. When our beliefs are challenged the Reactor App is tapped and an emotional peptide is released making us feel a specific way. This feeling is what distracts us away from our 'YOU' who knows everything.

6. We have an 'A' Switch. This is the awareness we can be, while we are reacting to our belief systems being challenged.

7. Once we flick the 'A' Switch we can acknowledge how amazingly powerful our peptides are and work out which belief system we have had challenged. This is when we can destroy the belief system so we no longer have to limit ourselves with it.

8. Remember we are Peptaholics. This means we are addicted to the emotional hit we are getting from our belief systems. We will always find ways to continue the story so we can continue taking the peptide hit.

Live a Life That is Limitless

9. Living from awareness and observation is 'THE NOW', the most powerful place we create our lives from. The 'Now', is the Moment we can become the Question and the Choice, not the Reaction and Distraction.

10. We ALWAYS have a choice.

11. What are you choosing NOW that will actualise abundance in all things?

12. We have been conditioned to do as we are told and give the right answer.
    When we have been conditioned to do as we are told, this creates the belief we don't have a choice. When we are conditioned to give the right answer this creates a belief we don't have any other choice but the Right one.

13. Would an infinite being not have a choice?

14. When we choose what is light for us it is a Truth for us and will be easy and light.

15. When we choose what feels heavy to us this is a Lie for us and will create difficulty and drama.

16. Always ask questions without trying to find the right answer.

17. Use What, Can and How to create your questions.
    What do I need to be aware of?
    Can I change this with ease?
    How do I change this with ease?

18. Use muscle testing to help you create awareness. Use closed questions and ask your body what he/she needs.

19. Don't judge others, observe and recognise the story they are playing out. Remember they are just reacting to the belief systems they hold, so you will be tempted to hook into the self judgement they are

Live a Life That is Limitless

projecting about themselves.

20. Don't Judge yourself. You will project your self judgement into the world for others to hook into. If you do this you will be judged, if you don't, you can't be judged.

21. Create vulnerability for yourself in your court room until the story you are playing out no longer causes you to react. Then say "JTFOOM".

22. Use JTFOOM everyday in every situation you find yourself. Imagine how people would be reacting around you if you just happened to be naked. Then JTFOOM!!! You will be surprised how much fun you can have with this, and how soon people can no longer judge you.

23. Stop waiting to be told what to do. You can choose anything and any questions now. What are you waiting for?
Ask: What choice, possibility and contribution can I be now?

John Swanepoel

Part Two

The Personal Focus System

CHAPTER TWENTY TWO

THE BRAIN IN GENERAL

The Left Brain and the Conscious Mind.

The left brain is the part of ourselves that creates and controls logical and rational thinking. It is the learning centre that receives and compiles new information in an ordered way. It provides us with logical explanations which helps us create practical and logical frameworks to interact with. It is the masculine aspect of ourselves which includes the Sympathetic Nervous System. Most schooling around the world uses linear learning methods to teach children. Linear learning helps us narrow our focus on a specific subject. The equivalent of a computer downloading files that can be integrated with existing files. The left brain is like a hard drive that stores information we have received in an ordered and rational way.

It organises the information into files and folders so we can find what we need easily. Like a reference library that enables us to access all we have learned.

When an athlete needs to learn a new technique, their coach will break the whole movement down into sections. This is the rational frame work that makes it easier for the athlete to make sense of the new information. Practicing each part of the movement or technique in the correct order, is the learning process we need to go through in order to create new pathways in the brain. Once the new sequence of movements has been repeated enough, the left brain can establish the new information in the long term memory. This is when the mental effort of rational mind can give way to what we call "second nature". This learning process is used for every aspect of our lives.

The Conscious Mind

The conscious mind is the like a 1GB receiver and processor of thought. It is limited by our belief systems and all the other peoples points of view we have aligned ourselves to. The conscious mind interprets the information

Live a Life That is Limitless

we receive from our five senses. Once processed, this information enables us to understand what is happening around us and defines how we see our environment and how we communicate with one another.

The conscious mind is where we make choices and is the most limiting aspect of ourselves. All information received by the conscious mind has been filtered through our belief systems, held in the part of the brain called the Cingulate Gyrus. This 1GB processor enables us to experience the information we receive through our emotions. Each emotion we experience is as a result of a peptide which has been created in the part of the brain call the Hypothalamus. As soon as the conscious mind becomes aware of a situation, the beliefs we hold about that situation will determine which peptide should be created and therefore how we feel. Our feelings are how we experience our world and how we react to it.

Our beliefs help us create the choices we make which make us feel the way we do at any given moment.

The Right Brain and the Sub Conscious Mind

The Right Brain is the assimilator of what has been learned by the left brain. The Right Brain is the part of ourselves that is our creativity and intuition. The "Felt Sense" which is described as the feminine aspect of ourselves. It incorporates the Parasympathetic Nervous system, the system that calms us down and allows us to relax. This part of our brain creates our ability to interpret information we receive through our subtle senses. It is the least logical part of ourselves which greatly increases our ability for creativity and expansive thinking. At the same time the right brain will access second nature information stored in our memory libraries. The right brain is how we think quickly and how sometimes we just know something without quite understanding how.

There are no limitations within Right Brain function. The Right Brain does not use the belief system filters in the Cingulate Gyrus. People who have developed their Right Brain abilities appear to be able to function at a far faster rate. Speed reading is an excellent example of this. When a person has mastered speed reading they have learned how to close down the left brain function and use a combination of "Second Nature" (already knowing how to read) and the Right Brain intuitive function. In this case the intuitive function enables the person to very quickly assimilate large chunks of text in a fraction of a second.

The Subconscious Mind.

The subconscious mind is the power house that runs the show. It is the many levels of our subconscious mind that keeps everything working in total harmony through our body/mind. Like a quantum mainframe that is so powerful it has to create programmes small enough for the conscious mind to understand.

The subconscious mind has been described as having four parts: The subconscious (Right Brain), sub of subconscious (Right Brain and Aorta), sub of super conscious (Heart Brain - Bio Field) and the super conscious state (Sola Plexus - Bio Field - Source Field). It operates like a massive mainframe that has no limitations, plugging us straight into the Source Field. It is the Right Brain functions and its interaction with the subconscious mind that you will be developing during PFS.

CHAPTER TWENTY THREE

States of Mind

Our mind has a number of states which are determined by the frequency of our brain activity. These are measured in cycles per second (c.p.s.).

BETA.
As mentioned above the conscious mind helps us interpret the world around us. The conscious mind is our everyday awake state, known as the BETA State which is usually measured from upwards of 14 c.p.s.

Live a Life That is Limitless

ALPHA

The Alpha state is measured at approximately 7 - 13 c.p.s. The Alpha state is the state when we are very relaxed but not asleep. The time just before we drift off to sleep when we are still thinking with clarity, or just before we open our eyes in the morning. We can achieve the Alpha state anywhere and at anytime. It is generally the time when we get our best ideas and clarity. That's the way we bypass the limitations of the left brain and tap into the creativity of the right. The Alpha state can be achieved while still conducting everyday activities. This is the state we are after when using PFS. You will learn how to come in and out of this state during this PFS foundation workshop.

THETA

The Theta state measures at approximately 4 - 6 c.p.s. This is also known as rapid eye movement phase of sleep. The time when we have just lost consciousness and fallen into a light sleep or are emerging from the Delta phase. This is the phase when we dream.

DELTA

The Delta state is the deepest level of sleep up to 4 c.p.s, when our bodies heal and repair. The brain for the first two hours and the rest of the body for the next two hours. After the four hour period we generally come back up to the Theta State.

The Alpha Mind

The Alpha mind (7 - 13 c.p.s.) is how we are able to tap into collective consciousness with clarity using visualisation. Collective consciousness has been described in many ways. The Hive Mind, Universal Consciousness, The Field, The Source Field, God Consciousness to name a few. We are continuously using the collective conscious mind, most of the time without being aware of it. There is plenty of documented research that confirms the existence of this and that we are all seemingly connected by it. The alpha mind is able by design, to tap into all levels of the subconscious simultaneously. Like accessing the universal library that holds all the information that has ever been and will ever be. Some of the greatest minds known to us Einstein, Beethoven, Newton, all used the alpha state to create and understand the information they received.

PFS is of course not a new or untested concept. The modern day interpretations of visualisation originate from the late 1970's when remote viewing was being developed by the CIA and KGB to spy on one another. The project was stopped by the US Government in the late eighties. It wasn't until the information was declassified at the turn of the century that people realised how accurate the system was. One remote viewer described a five story building next to the Kremlin in great detail. When the satellite photos of the area at the time were checked, there was no such building. Many years later when the same documents were studied after declassification, the building had been built and was described in perfect detail. This not only demonstrates the accuracy and validity of visualisation, it also gives us a good insight into the construct of time.

Once we are comfortable accessing the Alpha State, and we understand that time does not exist there, we can begin to develop an awareness of the alternative potential we have. The only thing that will hold us back is Judgement through the beliefs and points of view we have aligned and agreed with or resisted and reacted too, that do not serve us.

CHAPTER TWENTY FOUR

Visualisation, Imagination and the Pineal

Visualising is how we recall and replay memories that have been experienced using our mind. When we visualise past experiences we incorporate how the situation felt, looked like, sounded like. Sometimes we will remember how things smelt and tasted. The physiological mechanism of visualisation is still not fully understood, however

Live a Life That is Limitless

research over the past twenty years has helped us gain a clearer understanding of what is most likely happening during visualisation. Rather than focusing on the "Visual" to begin with we should acknowledge that not everyone uses their subtle senses in the same way. The felt sense still consists of the five senses of sight, sound, touch, taste and smell. The subtle senses are described as Clairvoyance (vision or imagination), Clairsentience (touch), Clairaudience (hearing), Clairalience (smell), Clairgustance (taste) and the sixth sense being Claircognizance (knowing).

I have not met anyone personally who uses subtle sense of smell or taste as a dominant sense. Saying that, there will be people who do. Most of us use a combination of Clairvoyance (visualisation or imagination), Clairsentience (Kinesthetics and touch) and Claircognisance (knowing). I have met one or two people who receive information through Clairaudience (auditory, hearing).

When we use our imagination we are still creating mental imagery but can change the story. So we might visualise how our bed room used to be like in the house we lived in when we were nine. We can then imagine what the room would look like if we changed the colour of the walls and furniture. So your Imagination always runs through the filters of your Left Brain.

Once in the Alpha state, follow what feels natural to you. If you can recall a memory of something you have done and you can sense exactly how it felt to move or stand, you favour the kinaesthetic and the subtle sense of touch. You know how a movement would feel to your body. People who know how their body will feel in a specific position, may not necessarily be able to see a clear picture in their mind of the position their body was in the memory. People who can visualise and imagine a past experience with clarity, tend to be able to visualise a clear picture in their mind of that experience. However it does not necessarily mean they can sense how, what they are visualising, would feel to their bodies.

Scientists now suspect that visualisation happens in the Pineal Gland in the centre of the brain. This has been referred to in every civilisation as the "Third Eye" and depicted as a pine cone. We now know the inner lining of the Pineal has the same light sensitive cones as the back of

Live a Life That is Limitless

our retinas. We also know fluid filling the gland is full of micro piezoluminescent Calcite crystals. These Calcite micro crystals light up when non electromagnetic information hits them. Piezoluminescence is present in similar forms in nature. Deep sea marine life use the same mechanism to light their environment. The luminescence produced is in the blue/green light spectrum and does not need heat (blood flow) to create the light.

The Calcite Micro-crystals are said to have their own Piezoelectric effect that is responsive to electromagnetic energies outside the physical body, and can also produce its own electromagnetic energy. A new form of bio-mineralization has been studied in the human Pineal Gland using scanning electron microscopy and energy dispersive spectroscopy.

Another substance that is produced in the Pineal is DMT (Dimethyltryptamine) which has been described as the spirit molecule. The human body is flooded with this substance at birth and at death, and at the 13th week of gestation of a human child - coinciding with the Tibetan Book of the Dead, referring to the exact time of when a soul can reincarnate in a new body on earth. It is found in many species of plants that are commonly used as hallucinogens in South American shamanic practice.

The non electromagnetic information in our case is thought to be the information we receive from the Source Field which we can tap into in the Alpha state. So maybe the combination of the piezoelectric crystals displaying the electromagnetic information pulsing through our environment and the DMT allowing a glimpse into realms beyond our 3D world is what gives us the opportunity to tap infinite potential through visualisation.

Interesting Facts about the Pineal

1. Pineal is the largest reservoir for Serotonin in the body.

2. Melatonin is produced in the Pineal which helps you sleep.

3. Fluoride not only damages the tissues of the pineal, it also furs up the calcite crystals preventing piezoluminescence.

Live a Life That is Limitless

4. Mobile communication frequencies disrupt the calcite crystals preventing piezoluminescence, as well as disrupting pineal function, causing altered energy patterns within the body and brain. This can effect the central nervous system, sexual function, sleep cycles or cause sleep deprivation.

5. Infra red energy bands disrupt the calcite crystals and piezoluminescence, causing sleepiness, crying, agitation, depression, anxiety, aggression, fear, terror, hopelessness, grief, apathy and even death. Lower frequency waves like infra red correspond to lower emotional moods. While higher frequency waves such as those in the green, blue and violet range produce higher emotional energies and moods. (Preston B. Nichols The Montauk Project copyright © 1992.)

CHAPTER TWENTY FIVE

The Alpha Zone: scepticism is wilful ignorance.

Remember in the Alpha Zone you can never be wrong....

The information we have covered up until now has been given to help you develop the fundamentals of visualisation techniques with as little distraction as possible. The distraction is from the reactions we get caught by every day. The disruption always comes from the Left Brain. Our Left Brain will always interfere with the visualisation process until we can preoccupy it enough to allow the Right Brain to function with more clarity. The Exercises in

Live a Life That is Limitless

this chapter and subsequent chapters are given for this reason.

Our Left Brain is constantly occupied through reason, belief systems and how we have been conditioned. We have been conditioned to find the right answer all the time. So as mentioned earlier we are always trying to find the right answer from our current knowledge base. The Left Brain holds the filter we see our world through. Everyone has different filters, no one will see the world in the same way as you do. No one sees you the way you see yourself.

The Alpha mind is the incredibly powerful, creative, intuitive and unstructured Right Brain. In PFS we create The Alpha Zone with parameters and structure. These parameters and structure are what allows you to access any information you seek and to create your spaces exactly as you need them to be. The library card to the infinite library of knowledge we have all been issued with. The effectiveness of your Alpha Zone will be based on the way you create it in the alpha state. As long as you access your Alpha Zone on occasion, you will retain it your whole life.

By creating an Alpha Zone with as much detail as possible you begin to preoccupy the left brain with the detail. Like planning and building a new home. Or redecorating a room. We give these things a lot of thought. We test different colours for the walls, choose matching colours for the windows. Find furnishings that suit the new decor and so on. Once the process is complete and we are satisfied, we use the room without taking too much notice of the decor and how it looks because we have achieved the look we were after. Some of us change the furniture around every now and then. Others leave the room as it is until they die or move house. Either way the left brain has been satisfied at the point of completing the room. All the justifications have been made for the colours and furnishing and the room is complete. We can then relax and enjoy the atmosphere and focus on other things without thinking about decorating it again.

This is no different when developing your Personal Focus System. Once your areas are complete you can relax and focus on creating new awarenesses in your world, you would not have otherwise considered possible.

Live a Life That is Limitless

The Alpha Zone is the where you will create, that will be the visualisation development centre in your own mind. A place that with practice can be accessed easily during any time of day or night, in the Beta and Alpha states, in any situation. You will learn to drop in and out of your Zone anytime, and use the Zone to hold interviews with others, build new and exciting relationships, repair damaged relationships, create wealth and maintain excellent health. Your intuition and subtle senses will heighten to levels you would not have believed possible while your left brain continues to play in the visual construct you have created for it.

CHAPTER TWENTY SIX

Using the Alpha State

As mentioned earlier, the Alpha state is the state when we are very relaxed but not asleep. The time just before we drift off to sleep when we are still thinking with clarity, or as we wake just before we open our eyes in the morning. As I said before, we can achieve the Alpha state anywhere and at anytime. Our best and clearest ideas come from the time we spend in the alpha zone. In the alpha zone we have circumvented the left brain limitations and this provides us access to the creativity of the right.

To achieve the Alpha State you can use any relaxation technique that works for you. Most people who are reading this book will have at some time or another learnt a relaxation method they use. If you have ever been taught meditation, you may find the processes they go through

Live a Life That is Limitless

to find inner quiet, work well here to.

Stage 1

Relaxing the body and mind.

Find a place where you will not be disturbed for at least 20 minutes. Adopt a comfortable supported position either on the ground or in a chair. In the early stages of learning to use the Alpha State avoid lying on your bed. This will reduce the chances of you falling asleep during the exercise.

Once you are comfortable, close your eyes and take five long slow deep breaths in through the nose and out through your mouth. Once you have completed your breath sequence start from your head and work systematically down through your body. Tense all the major muscles groups one by one. Hold your contractions for a slow count to three and then release. Start with the head and face muscles, neck and shoulders. Then gradually move through the chest and upper back, abdomen and lower back, pelvis, buttocks and upper legs, lower legs and finally your feet. As you relax from your contractions, breathe out and feel your body sink into the floor or chair.

Allow yourself to be totally supported. Every joint and muscle. Feel the tension release from your body and dissipate through the ground beneath you.

Continue focusing on every part of your body in the same top to bottom sequence. The second time instead of contractions, notice how each part of the body you are focusing on feels when it is totally supported. Floating, held up by the floor or chair you are in. Once you have completed the second circuit from head to foot you will be either in or nearing the Alpha state. The more you practice this sequence with no distraction the easier it will become.

Stage 2

Visualisation, Imagination and the Subtle Senses.

You may remember earlier in the book I mentioned the subtle senses and how once in the Alpha state, you should find what is natural for you. This is where you will develop a better understanding of which of the subtle senses you favour. During this phase you will also develop the weaker senses and establish new neurological path-

Live a Life That is Limitless

ways in the brain that improve your ability to visualise with more clarity.

Once you have achieved the Alpha State, keeping your eyes closed, begin to visualise the colour red. Visualising is not seeing with your eyes. Don't try and see the colour red. You can't, your eyes are closed. Remember Visualisation is recalling how something looks using your mind not your eyes. If you are finding it difficult to create a mental image of a colour or object start using your imagination.

Imagination is not visualisation. When we visualise we are viewing a mental image of something we have physically seen or imagined previously. When we use our imagination we are creating a new mental image we have not seen before.

So we can visualise how the room we decorated looks through a mental image memory of the colour of the walls, furnishings and layout within the room. When we use our imagination we create a new mental image of how the room might look with a different colour paint, furnishings and layouts. Imagination becomes visualisation as soon as you return to a mental image you previously created using your imagination.

Visualisation is a mental image of how something is, or how a mental image shows up without a point of view attached.

Imagination is a mental image that has been created through the limitations of the left brain and the Interesting Thoughts and points of view we create from the belief systems we hold.

When we can visualise something with no point of view attached, we can start to actualise the mental imagery we are visualising in our everyday lives.

Start by focusing on things that are familiar to you. For red, visualise a strawberry, red apple, red car or glass of red wine. This helps you start to build the path ways in the brain that will develop clarity. Once you have started visualising red and you have a clear mental image, start to imagine what red tastes like, sounds like, feels like and smells like. Take your time with this part of the exercises. If red was behind you what would it feel like and how would you know it was red.

This is when your left brain will be throwing IT's into the mix. Acknowledge the Interesting Thoughts that wash through your mind about how red should or should not be.

Live a Life That is Limitless

What ever shows up is OK. Go with it. You are never wrong when visualising or imagining.

Once you have completed all the aspects of red move on through the spectrum to orange, yellow, green, blue, purple and indigo. Take your time with each colour. Go through all the five senses with each colour until you have a mental image of each colour with ease and clarity.

Don't be put off by time.

At this point in developing your visualisation skills don't be put off by the fact that you seem to be taking ages to visualise a colour. Time is a construct and can only exist as long as it is being observed. Time, as you will come to realise very soon, does not exist in the Alpha Zone. If you don't have the time in your day to take 30 minutes to an hour to practice, break everything down into 10 or 15 minute slots. Practice going into the Alpha State and focus on the colour your are having most difficulty creating a mental image of. Commit to making the time just before you go to bed or early in the morning before you start your day. Once you have established clarity with all the colours of the spectrum you will begin to be able to visualise and imagine with ease and clarity.

CHAPTER TWENTY SEVEN

Through the vale into your garden

Once you have completed the spectrum colours, visualise yourself pulling all the colours together to form a vale of white light. Like a thick curtain. Imagine yourself stepping through the curtain into your garden.

In the garden you will have to use your imagination to begin with as you will have never been there before. Create a place where you can totally relax and enjoy your surroundings. This is a place unique to you where no one else will ever go. This is your place for peace and relaxation. A sanctuary that can be anywhere. As you visualise yourself stepping through the white vale into the garden, allow whatever shows up to evolve in your imagination. Are you in the woods, on a hill, by a river or on a beach? Go with what shows up. Remember your left brain will be

Live a Life That is Limitless

throwing ideas and odd things at you because it likes to be in control.

Look around your garden and take note of everything. You can choose how you would like it to look. The grass, trees, water, flowers. Where are they, what do they feel like, smell like and sound like? Are there insects or other wild life around? What are they doing? Look closely at the colours and textures of everything in your garden. You are still developing the spectrum colours at this stage, so are establishing stronger neurological pathways in the brain that will ultimately enhance the mental imagery you get.

Find a place where you can relax. Sit a while and observe the layout of your garden. Familiarise yourself with every nook and cranny. While you are in your garden focusing on the things around you, you will have IT's drifting through your mind. Imagine yourself plucking each thought from your mind and placing it somewhere in the garden. Some people like to float their IT's down a stream or blow them away in the wind. Find what works for you and keep your focus on allowing all thoughts to be passed away. Say thank you to your left brain for its contribution and continue focusing on all the interesting things that show up in your garden.

CHAPTER TWENTY EIGHT

Creating Your Alpha Zone

Your alpha zone is the place you will visually construct with a number of rooms and areas that can be used to focus on specific aspects of your life. It is important to mime all movements during the construction phase. Work as thoroughly as you can. Use an open plan space you can move comfortably about in.

The Alpha Zone Entrance Way

To start this phase use the relaxation techniques you have practiced to get you back into the Alpha State. Once you are in your garden and relaxed, stand up in the centre of your chosen physical work space. Keep your eyes closed and mind focused on the mental imagery of your garden. Choose a place in your garden where you can create an entrance to your Alpha Zone.

Live a Life That is Limitless

Use your imagination. How will your entrance look? Will there be stairs or a path? What material will you use to construct the entrance? What tools will you need? Take your time and imagine or visualise the tools and the materials. Where will you store them while you are using them? Do you even need a storage area or is everything just showing up as it is needed. As you start constructing the entrance to your Alpha Zone using your mental imagery, physically mime the movements you are seeing in your mind. Do the actions. Imagine the sound, weight, texture and smell of the materials you are using.

Once you have completed your pathway or stairs, create a small court yard. Go through the same physical and mental procedures with everything

you do. Take your time, this is where you can really start to develop the subtle Visual, Kinaesthetic, Auditory, Taste and Smell senses.

This is the first stage in constructing a mental imagery tool that you will be able to use for the rest of your life. The beginning of developing you visualisation as a powerful tool you will use to actualise your life in any way you choose.

Some people get impatient during this phase of creating and establishing their Alpha Zone. This is understandable considering the amount of noise your left brain will kick up around what is possible and what isn't. Remember your conditioning and the hidden small print that will always hold you back, like someone always telling you that you can't do something. Remember, those who say something is impossible, only do so because they believe they would never be able to achieve it. This is why scepticism is wilful ignorance. It is a disregard of our greatest gift. The ability to receive any answer from the infinite library we have access to, through asking questions without trying to find the right answer.

There is no right or wrong way to construct your Alpha Zone. Go with what shows up, what ever pops into your head first is OK. Allow the space to evolve without resistance. Take your time, the more detail you create through every stage of your Alpha Zone construction the clearer your mental clarity and intuition will become.

Live a Life That is Limitless

The Court Yard and Your Secret Door.

Your entrance way will open out onto a court yard. As with your entrance way, create a courtyard anyway you choose. Once you have established and built your courtyard, choose the location on the edge of your court yard where you would like to create your main building. Construct the outer wall of your main building. Next to the wall create a large container. Fit your container with a lid and in the lid create a small chimney. This is you first tool. Choose the area in your wall you would like your main door. This door is a secret door that can only be activated by you. Invisible until you are standing in front of it. Place a white light above the entrance and a sensor that reads your body and energy fields. There are no handles or buttons to this door, only the sensors that will open the door

for you once you stand in front of them. As the door opens, you will be bathed in white light as you pass across your thresh hold. Keep the detail up with your mental imagery. Visualise and imagine everything as clearly as you can. Remember if your mental imagery is still not very clear, continue to use your senses to sense how your new constructions are taking shape within your mind. Continue to develop your subtle senses by going through how everything might taste, smell, feel and sound.

CHAPTER TWENTY NINE

Entering and Constructing your Alpha Zone.

Your Interview Room.

Activate you secret door and cross the threshold through your white light. You are entering what will become your interview room. This is where you will be able to invite people into your Alpha Zone and interact with them energetically. Allow your room to evolve in your imagination. Remember to continually physically act out all movements during your construction, in the area you have cho-

Live a Life That is Limitless

sen to do your visualisation. Construct the shape of the room, walls floors and ceilings. Decorate the walls and floors with whatever comes to mind to make your interview room comfortable. Create a space you would be comfortable working and concentrating in.

The Lift

Once you have completed the first stage of your interview room choose the wall you would like to build a lift.

Construct your lift in the following way.

- The door should open by sliding from the top down.

- There should be a control tablet both on the outside and inside of the lift that can take all details. Names, dates, times and any location.

- Build a remote control tablet for your elevator that will be kept with you while you are in your Alpha Zone.

- Place a white light on the inside of your lift.

- Place a white light above the door on the outside of the lift.

Once your lift is complete, seal the area of the lift off using a glass wall with a sliding door that is connected to the control tablet you have. Build a turbo charged extractor in the ceiling behind the glass wall just above the entrance to the lift.

Test all gadgets in your Alpha Zone. All internal doors, tablets, extractor units. Step into your lift and test the door, make sure its working OK.

Fitting Out Your interview space

Your interview space is the area you have remaining in your interview room. Fit it out as you wish, have a comfortable seat and desk. Create a high definition screen on the wall that is like a huge electronic post it note pad. Create each screen with a frame that can be activated in either white or black light. On your desk, have a tablet that has a wifi access to your infinite library. Use any other tools you may have in a study or office you are familiar with and like to use. If you prefer pen and paper use that. Have a calendar and clock if you prefer those to a tablet that has all that information included. Have a video phone you can use to call any number in the world

Live a Life That is Limitless

with good connection. Link everything into your post-it screens. Remember to sense how everything smells, tastes, feels and sounds like as well as how it looks through you mental imaging.

Once you are happy with your interview room and all your tools, you will need to create three more areas that are accessed from your Interview room within your Alpha Zone. Build each room as you did your interview room. Walls, decor and fit out.

1. Relaxation Area.
   Your relaxation area should be luxurious and have anything in there you would love to have in your world you may not have yet. Perfect surroundings, hot pool, bar, library, swimming pool, large deck, beautiful views. Whatever shows up in your Alpha Zone that would be fantastic for you to be able to experience and create a place of total relaxation for you. You are alone, you don't have anyone in your space with you yet, so only things you would find relaxing if you were alone.

2. Healing Room.
   This is a special and powerful room. A place where

the most important aspect of our physical being can be effectively addressed. Without our health we have no quality of life. Money and relationships mean little when we don't have good health. Once you have built your walls and decorated them you will need to create a healing tool. This is an object that has the ability to vibrate at any level. Allow your object to show up. Let it be as it first shows up. It is the kind of thing that is unique to you. When you hold it over your body and activate it, your healing tool will do whatever your body needs to heal itself. It doesn't matter how it looks or feels. Remember you can't be wrong when using visualisation and imagination. Once your tool is constructed create a bed to lie on and a pull down, full body scanning screen that is linked to your control tablet. Test all your health equipment. How does your body look in your screen once you have scanned yourself. How does your healing tool work and how comfortable is the bed in your healing room.

3. Body Conditioning Room
This room is like a gym or exercise training area. If you are an athlete, what kind of equipment do you

Live a Life That is Limitless

need for your specific discipline. For high performance athletes this is a MUST room to have. Every piece of equipment you could possibly imagine can be included here. From an Olympic size pool to a rugby field, running track or 10m diving board, anything is possible.

As mentioned earlier in the book, there is plenty of evidence that proves the parietal lobes are activated in the same way during actual physical movement as they are when you visualise or imagine a movement. It is as if your brain doesn't know the difference between actual physical movement and visualisation of movement. This means the same neurological pathways are being established in the somatosensory cortices during both physical movement and visualisation of physical movements.

This works for everyone no matter what their physical ability. This phenomenon can also be used to help people recover movement pat

terns after they have been seriously injured.

If you just use exercise for fun to stay healthy, fit your conditioning room out with equipment you are familiar with. If you don't like gyms, create a space where you can exercise doing the things you enjoy the most. Swimming, running, walking, biking, climbing etc.

CHAPTER THIRTY

Using Your Alpha Zone

This section is best taught in a workshop environment. Look out for Personal Focus System workshop dates in your area on my website at www.johnswanepoel.com If you like what you have read so far, and would like a position coordinating workshops in your country, area, university or school. Contact me via the website for information on availability and commissions.

Live a Life That is Limitless

Question: What vibration can I become now that will actualise '<u>everything I am choosing</u>' instantly and with total ease?

(if you are going to ask this question, make sure you define what you are choosing is a truth for you. Remember choosing what is Light is your Truth)

Your Lift

The lift is one of the most fun tools you have in your alpha zone. Follow the protocol carefully to get the most accurate results. Never hold a point of view about anything that happens in your Alpha State. Remember to acknowledge the Left Brain and thank it for all the IT's it will throw your way during any exercise you conduct in your Alpha Zone. Having no point of view about any of the interference will hold you in Observation far longer. This is where you are not reacting to any point of view that shows up. Observing with no reaction or control over how things show up will actualise what you are visualising. When something shows up in a way you were not expecting ask questions and wait to see what changes that question will create. Keep asking until you become aware of the answer that feels the lightest too you.

Then ask: What vibration do I need to be to actualise ……. now?

Inviting guests to your Alpha Zone.

Time does not exist in the Alpha Zone, so you have to create the exact coordinates for the time you wish to work in when inviting a guest into your Alpha Zone. When a guest shows up, it is their hologram as it would present at the time you have stipulated on your tablet control for your lift. If you invite someone in without including specific details of time and dates they can show up at any stage in their life, or not at all. An individual will only show up if they choose to energetically. If the person you have chosen does not show up in your lift that's ok. Try a different date/time or leave it for a couple of days and try again. If you are at odds with someone who is refusing to meet up with you in person, they may still show up energetically if you invite them in.

Live a Life That is Limitless

When someone shows up you should invite them to stand under the white light at the entrance to the lift for a while and see if their hologram changes in anyway. Once everything has settled, invite them to step into the area behind the glass wall and welcome them into your space. You can conduct your meeting with the glass wall between you and them or invite them to join you in your space. Choose which is most comfortable for you.

Always be polite and the perfect host no matter how you feel about them. Make them comfortable and ask questions. Observe how they behave. Tell them why you have invited them in and what you are expecting to achieve from the meeting.

You will need to acknowledge how you use you visualisation and recognise how you will most likely receive information. Which of your subtle senses have you developed the most during the construction phase of your Alpha Zone. When I started people used to show me things and point at things until I developed the sentient aspect of my intuition. Now I just get the information as a knowing and visual demonstration. I see what is going on and ask questions around what I need to be aware of and what I need to do to create change with ease.

If your guest is ill and you would like to contribute to their recovery, invite them into your healing room to relax. You can work on them there, even if you have no health care knowledge.

Would an infinite being not know how to heal?

Ask:
How can I contribute to this persons healing now and in the future?

What do I need to be aware of that will help this person heal?

Inviting people into you interview area is also extremely effective for business meetings and dealing with work colleagues. Keeping the right people informed subconsciously about your intentions can help situations progress smoothly within groups and organisations, as well as create awareness of what may be happening that you have not been aware of.

Live a Life That is Limitless

Inviting the best person into your Alpha Zone

If you are stuck and don't know of anyone who you could invite into your Alpha Zone who would be able to help with a particular problem, type the following into your control tablet, or say:

I invite the best person at this moment in time to help me with…..

Go with whatever or whoever shows up. Go through the white light protocol and find out who they are and what they do. If you are not comfortable with how they show up, invite them politely to leave via the lift. If they refuse or mess around, ask: Where will you be in the future? and hit your extractor unit button. Watch the hologram disappear through your roof to wherever they will be in the future. I have never had to do this.

If you wish to invite someone in who you know has died, make sure you use coordinates for when they were alive. Their hologram only exists till the time of their death so they only know what they knew until that moment. I have never purposely invited anyone who has passed. I don't have a need to do that. If someone shows up who has passed and who is the best person to help me out at this moment in time, so be it. I will welcome them in with open arms and listen to/observe everything they have to show me.

Remember this is your Alpha Zone. You have control over everything that happens there. No-one can harm you ... it's in your head. Use the tools as described and you will experience everything with clarity. and above all have fun.

Using your lift to explore places.

You can explore anywhere in the universe from your lift. Type in the coordinates you wish to visit, step into you lift and go there. Your coordinates can be a physical address of someone's home, or a building you would like to see the inside of. You will need the address, date and time you wish to go to. Remember time doesn't exist in the Alpha Zone so be accurate.

You will always see the places you go to through your own filters (Left Brain) until you have developed your visualisation skills to a much deeper level. During one of my early workshops I took my students to the classroom we

Live a Life That is Limitless

were using, two weeks ahead. I asked them to walk into the class room at 8pm on that specific date and check the far corner for an item. They had to describe the item in as much detail as possible. They all swopped notes without discussing anything they had visualised. Two weeks later at 8pm we read each note out to the class. One third of the class picked up items that were in the corner. The main one was a red shoe box I had brought in that evening before the class started. A couple of students picked out the box, one person described one of the items in the box and one picked out the porcelain dishes that were stored in the cupboard the box was sitting on. The exercise was done in the fourth week of a ten week workshop so it was early days in developing their visualisation skills. Everyone improved by the end of the course. Don't be put off. Always go back to the basics of the spectrum colours, garden and building phases. Once you silence your Left brain with the detail you create in your Alpha Zone you will be able to visualise with more clarity.

JTFOOM!!!

Using your lift to take you to your court room
Your lift is the perfect tool to use with your court room.

Working through the embarrassing choices we have made in our lives is one of the ways mentioned in part 1 that will make JTFOOM a very powerful tool for you. Once we no longer judge ourselves we can't be judged.

Use your court to take yourself to court. Include anyone you would feel uncomfortable finding out about your little secret. Put yourself on trial without saying sorry. Be humble through the process. Admit the choices you made where not the best at the time and then allow yourself to be judged. Then JTFOOM the whole scene. Keep going back to the court room until you no longer have a reaction to the story.

Using Your Post-It Screen

Your Post-it screen is used to see how things might turn out. When you are developing your visualisation use your screen to show you different scenes. Practice by turning on the screen and viewing a familiar scene. Use your remote control to fast forward through the picture and see what shows up. One of the best exercises is to put a movie of your garden up on the screen and then fast for-

Live a Life That is Limitless

ward through the seasons and observe how your garden changes.

Turn on your screen and ask questions about specific things or subjects. Watch scenarios play out and ask to be shown how different scenarios would work out if you made different choices.

A scenario can be anything, relationships, money or health orientated. If you would like to create and actualise something new. Turn on the white frame that lights up the outside of your screen.

Ask questions that will actualise what you would like to create. There are no limitations in the Alpha Zone anything is possible.

If you would like to leave a part of your life behind that is still playing a significant role in pulling you into reaction. Turn on the black frame light you have around your screen and play the whole story out on your screen. Once it is finished, peel the post-it screen off the wall, role it up and go out onto your courtyard. Open the incinerator and place the screen at the bottom. Set it alight and close the lid with the chimney. Let it burn till there is nothing left.

Never think of or play that story again. If it ever pops up again, through other people, ask them for their side of the story and do the same thing again with their story. The black screen is there to destroy and uncreate anything that has held you back or continues to hold you back and create trauma and drama in your life.

While using your screen ask:

Where am I mimicking my parents and how is it holding me back?

How am I measuring how well I am mimicking my parents and what do I need to be aware of to change this?

Put the story on the black boarder screen and burn it.

Using your tablet and other tools.

Tablets and computers are pretty much the same thing. Use these to get information like you would do ordinarily. Type in questions and see what shows up. This is like a direct link in to the infinite library we mentioned before. Using these tools is just a more familiar way of accessing

Live a Life That is Limitless

information than playing stories on a screen or getting in a lift and exploring.

You can have video calls with people too. Remember to type in all coordinate before you start calling them. Let them show up on the screen as they choose.

Every time you enter your Alpha Zone you will improve your ability to visualise and actualise. Create any tool for you that you believe will work for you.

Using Your Healing Room.

The healing room can be used exclusively for you or you can open it up to people you have invited into your Alpha Zone. On the controls for your drop down scanning screen, put all the categories of the body. Organs, Endocrines, body parts. Include circulatory systems (blood), musculoskeletal system, filtrations systems (Lymph), and the nervous system. When you use your screen push the button of the system you wish to use and scan that part of your body with your screen. Take a look at what shows up. How does your body look? Most people see shadows over areas. The clarity of how you see your body will have a direct link to how much anatomical knowledge you have. Remember there are no mistakes, you are just seeing things through your filters. Apply your healing tool over the areas that show up in your body scan. Ask what do I need to perceive, know be and receive now that will heal these parts of my body. What vibration do I need to be that will reverse and destroy this pathology.

Cancer.
First Ask: What is the value in dying?

Breast cancer:
What is the value in mutilating myself to force someone else to step up?
What am I not willing to receive?
Where am I resenting not being acknowledged?

Colon cancer:
What is the value in mutilating myself to keep control?
What am I not willing to let go of?

Pancreatic cancer:
What is the value in worrying about grief?
What grief am I not willing to release?

Lung cancer:
What fear am I not willing to release?

Live a Life That is Limitless

Parkinson's:
What is the value in changing the way I move?

Recurring musculoskeletal injuries.
What aspect of my biotensegrity that needs to be released has been over looked?

General:
What aspect of having this illness am I addicted too? (Addiction is just a belief you don't have a choice)
What do I need to be aware of to help others recover from the same condition I have recovered from?

Money and Receiving

Your Glass Ceiling.
Most people have a hidden ceiling that defines how much money they can receive with ease. Most people are not even aware of this in their lives. One of the best examples of this glass ceiling with money is an experience I had with a business woman I was working with a few years ago. She was, and still is a successful business woman who owns a business sales agency. Let's call her Debbie.

We started by finding out how much money Debbie could loose without freaking out. This scenario can be played out any way that works for the individual. Similar to the Court Room, find a story that pushes your Reactor Apps. Debbie used a scenario where she destroyed her hard earned cash until she started to feel uncomfortable. The maximum figure she could shred with ease was $30K.

Debbie then wanted to know the relevance of this scenario. I pointed out that one can receive with ease the amount they can lose with ease. Anything over and above that amount tends to get used up, usually unnecessarily. She smiled and told me about her latest business deal.

Only a few weeks previously she had managed to sell the most expensive business on her books. She felt the 10% commission which is the industry standard was rude, so dropped her commission rate to 7%. She was shocked when she realised the gross sum she received in commissions was $30K. Which obviously turned out to be far less after taxes. She could receive anything up to $30K with ease. Anything over that figure created a discomfort for her subconsciously. She then adjusted her commission as

Live a Life That is Limitless

she was unable to receive over and above her glass ceiling with ease. She even created a situation for herself that ensured she wouldn't get too close to her maximum figure of 30K by making sure she had far less after taxes.

I also learned my hidden ceiling was far less. When I was 14years old my family emigrated to the UK from Zimbabwe. At the time people leaving the country were only allowed to take $2K Zimbabwean dollars with them. Everything else had to be left in the country. My mother is English so we had English Patriality. My parents walked into a job in the UK so $2K in those days was enough to get you started as a Zimbabwean dollar had the same value as a UK Pound. Subconsciously I had registered that as long as I have 2K I'll be fine.

One of the reasons this hidden ceiling is so strong is the Judgments we have of ourselves. Receiving belongs to the earth element in Traditional Chinese Medicine. It belongs to the Spleen in the body which represents three things. Spleen, Pancreas and Thymus. The spleen governs the immune system and the lymphatics of the body. The aspects of consciousness behind the earth element are:

worry thinking, ability to receive, consciousness of self worth, heart protection and defensive patterns.

When we are judging ourselves to be not good enough and are not allowing ourselves to receive, we are choking the flow of all receiving. If we do receive an amount over and above our glass ceiling because we have judged ourselves unworthy (consciousness of self worth) we will usually find a way of getting rid of the excess cash.

Discomfort with money.

"Money is the root of all Evil" is an example of a perpetual lie that has been conditioned into our society. The judgement that money is evil limits the flow and underpins the reasoning we make for not having too much money in our lives. Lies like that actually create a consciousness of disdain towards money. Money is a form of energy. It is the choices people make around money that creates the trauma and drama we associate with not having enough.

"People who are millionaires are greedy and tight with money".

Live a Life That is Limitless

"I don't need that much money".
"If I won Lotto I'd give most of it away".

These are examples of the limiting judgements about money that are floating around in society. The lie creates a dislike of money. When we dislike money we only create enough to get by. Or we create plenty of money at a price; The price of hard work, becoming a slave to money.

Money is just energy. As long as there are no blocks to the flow you can create as much or as little as you need whenever you need it. It is the discomfort of having money that chokes the flow for most people. Three ways to overcome this discomfort are as follows:

> Identify the lie that is your glass ceiling.
> As mentioned above

> Pay yourself first.
> Pay yourself first before anyone else. Take the top 10% and put it in a savings account never to be touched. This begins to change your consciousness of self worth, and creates a system where you allow

yourself to receive. The more money you accumulate the more money you are allowing yourself to have. The closer you get to your glass ceiling the stricter you need to become. Once you exceed the ceiling lock your savings away in an account you can't get your hands on very easily and continue adding your 10% regularly. This will help smash the ceiling for good and create and ease with having money in your world. With the current financial climate you could choose to buy precious metals with your ten percent. That way you create solid wealth that is controlled by you and not a bank.

Carry cash.
Always carry an amount of cash in your wallet that makes you feel a little uncomfortable. Zip it away in the back of your wallet and never touch it. This develops your allowance with money. You start to allow yourself to have more money in your life. If you lose your wallet, that's OK too. That is an opportunity to create more in your life; you have just created a huge space that can be refilled with even more money. When the front of your wallet is empty of cash and

Live a Life That is Limitless

you don't have much left in the bank, you will always be assured you still have money. This takes the fear away of not having enough. Creates a reassurance and a platform to create even more in your life.

Use your lift to invite the best person at this moment in time to help you with your finances.

Pick some of the questions below. Choose the ones you would least like to ask.

30 Questions you can ask about money:
1. What is my glass ceiling for money?
2. How do I destroy my glass ceiling for money?
3. How do I create more ease and joy with money?
4. What caused my dislike of money?
5. What do I need to be aware of that will change the way I make money?
6. What other ways are there to receive money I am not aware of?
7. How can I receive obscene amounts of money with ease?

8. What do I need to be aware of to keep obscene amounts of money with ease?
9. How can I pull money to me?
10. How can I create an energy pull of money to me?
11. Where am I not allowing myself to receive money with ease?
12. What do I need to perceive know be and receive now that will enable me to have abundance with money?
13. Where am I not willing to give money away with ease?
14. What am I not willing to lose?
15. Where am I not willing to lose money?
16. What do I need to be aware of to be able to lose all my money with ease?
17. How do I create a perpetual flow of money through my life with ease?
18. How do I create a life of ease with money?
19. Where am I not valuing myself?
20. What can I do to change my limitations with money?
21. How do I create more possibilities for money to come to me?
22. What bullshit belief systems are causing me to worry about money?

Live a Life That is Limitless

23. How am I making myself unworthy of receiving obscene amounts of money for fun?
24. Where am I defending other people's points of view about money that are preventing total ease with money for me?
25. Where am I choosing to limit my ability to receive by believing I have to give back if I receive?
26. How am I allowing myself to be abused with money?
27. How am I using a lack of money to abuse myself and my family?
28. Where am I addicted to never having enough money?
29. How can I create more money in my business while working less hours with total ease?
30. How can I create total ease joy and fun with money for the rest of my life?

Relationships - Undoing the limitations of mimicry.

In the first nine years of your life you are in what some call the hypnogogic state. All this means is you are in download mode. Your body console is downloading everything that happens to you and in front of you. There is no conceptualisation during this phase of your life.

As adults we assume children understand our conceptualisation of the world because they are so good a mimicking us. They don't, all they do is download everything that happens to them and in front of them. Loving hugs, arguments, attitudes, movies, TV programmes, language, how you dress, get up in the morning, drink coffee, beer or wine. How you dance, laugh and cry, scream or shout.

One of my patients many years ago had survived a serious flying accident. He had been told he would never walk again. He told the doctor where to go, and proved everyone wrong. He needed extensive rehab and ended up walking by himself with a stick. a couple of years after his recovery he brought his eldest son to see me because he was concerned he wasn't walking properly and was experiencing recurring injuries in his lower limbs. On examination there was nothing wrong with the boy. We worked out he was mimicking his dad in the way he chose to move. His dad's accident happened when he was very young. Once we recognised this we changed his move-

Live a Life That is Limitless

ment patterns and he no longer created injuries in his lower limbs. This is unusual and a good example of how we mimic the people around us as we grow up.

Around your eighth year you begin to wake, have a snooze and a little lie in when you are nine and finally wake up to the world when you are about ten. Some people are snapped awake early because of high stress experiences, but most people go through this eight year download phase. We download the belief systems our parents have, their behaviours, mannerisms and aspects of their characters that are similar to ours and some that are totally alien to us. We begin to mimic them and those closest to us in our communities. When we wake up at ten, we continue mimicking those who have moulded us, and now we start measuring how well we are mimicking what we have downloaded. This is where we start to become self conscious and judge ourselves. It is a subconscious judgement at first, wondering if your mimicking is to a high enough standard. When you get to your teenage years you finally realise you would be happier with your own identity and begin to distance yourself from your parents. You don't have to do this anymore. Just recognise the discomfort you are experiencing is the lie of the mimicry. Everything you have downloaded that is a lie for you will create a Reaction. From sport, arts, academics, religion, health, and any other category that is relevant to your story. If something feels heavy to you it is a Lie. You are not here for the Lie you are here for your Truth.

Most of us are conditioned away from our Truth through education. This includes our parents and their parents, parents, parents sometimes back as far as seven generations. Time to break the conditioning by seeing it for what it is and creating and maintaining awareness by asking questions.

Choose the tool in your Alpha Zone you enjoy using the most. Start asking the questions below and see what shows up. Once you have an answer, ask if it needs to be destroyed. If you get a yes, destroy it completely using your black framed post-it screen, or the statement written below.

1. What is my Truth and what do I Love to do?

Live a Life That is Limitless

2. What mimicry am I using that is limiting me in my life?
3. How is the mimicry I am using distracting me from my Truth?
4. How am I holding myself from my Truth by judging my mimicry to be not good enough?
5. What Beliefs and Interesting Thoughts am I using to justify continuing to mimic everything that is a Lie for me?
6. What Beliefs and Interesting Thoughts am I Reacting to that are Distracting me from my Truth?
7. Where am I mimicking my parents in my <u>Relationship</u>?
8. What can I choose now that will not include mimicry and will be Light for me?
9. Where am I limiting myself by judging what I have downloaded in my first nine years to be right?
10. Where am I limiting myself by judging what I have downloaded in my first nine years to be wrong?
11. How am I limiting my ability to receive money through the mimicry I am choosing?
12. How am I limiting my ability to make money through the mimicry I am choosing?

13. How am I limiting my ability to have money through the mimicry I am choosing?
14. Where am I mimicking my parents in my <u>Health</u>?
15. What choice can I be now that will change my health now and in the future?
16. What mimicry am I using to choose how I heal?
17. What choice can I be now that will change the way I heal now and in the future?
18. What mimicry am I using to choose this pathology?
19. What choice can I be now that will destroy this pathology in my body now and in the future?

When an answer pops up or is shown to you in your Alpha Zone, you can use your muscle testing to help confirm if it needs to be destroyed completely.

Each time you become aware of an answer that needs to be destroyed say the following:

Destroy and uncreate this completely. All I see is me. I love you, I am sorry, please forgive me, thank you.

Live a Life That is Limitless

Remember, what you say, you create. When you say: Destroy and uncreate this completely, the aspect, Belief, or 'IT' will no longer exist anywhere.

Then you acknowledge that all you are seeing at any moment is you or an aspect within you, by saying:

ALL I SEE IS ME.

Once you have stated the focus is on you, you can use the Hoponopono Prayer on your body console:

I love you, I'm sorry, please forgive me, thank you.

This is just one way of helping you to clear the conditioning so you can start to actualise your life with more ease and awareness.

When we ask a question, we contract our reality to a point where we create a potential for limitless possibilities.

When we ask the question without trying to find the right answer, we release the potential of limitless possibilities.

When we allow ourselves to receive limitless possibilities we create the potential to live a life that is limitless.

When we choose from those possibilities that show up that are a Truth for us, we start actualising a life that is limitless.

Have fun with this system it will help you unstick aspects of your life that have been holding you back. Remember the ONLY thing that should be hard in life is a penis!! Everything else should be easy, challenging and light. Enjoy your life challenges, you always will when you are doing what is Light and a Truth for you. Above all have fun. I look forward to meeting you one day soon. You are amazing and dearly loved.

If LIMITLESS was easy what would you choose?

John Swanepoel

Live a Life That is Limitless

www.ingramcontent.com/pod-product-compliance
Lightning Source LLC
Chambersburg PA
CBHW051924160426
43198CB00012B/2028